Praise for *Flow Leadership*

'What makes FLOW@WORK so powerful and practical is Gaëlle's relatable story of navigating all of its well-researched concepts. And FLOW@WORK's concepts of enlightenment, well-being, joy, and emotional balance in work are needed now more than ever. Read this book and put it into action.'

—**Zach Mercurio, PhD,** author of *The Invisible Leader* and *The Power of Mattering*

'*Flow Leadership* is exactly what the corporate world needs right now. Gaëlle Devins expertly shows how a new approach to leadership – one that balances *People, Purpose and Performance* – can transform a business from the inside out. It's a must-read for any leader ready to embrace the future of work.'

—**John Gerzema,** CEO of The Harris Poll and NYT bestselling author

'In *Flow Leadership*, Gaëlle Devins offers a practical roadmap for leaders looking to unlock their team's true potential. By focusing on purpose and humanity, she redefines what success looks like in the modern workplace. This is the leadership guide we've been waiting for.'

—**Jeremy Gutsche,** CEO of Trend Hunter and NYT bestselling author

'*Flow Leadership* is a game-changer for modern leaders. What sets this book apart is its remarkably practical approach to transforming workplace culture. Unlike many leadership books that stay in the realm of theory, Devins provides concrete tools and frameworks you can implement immediately. The book's real strength lies in how it breaks down complex concepts into actionable steps. For instance, the chapter on translating company values into behavioral principles includes specific methods for running workshops and implementing change. I especially appreciated the practical templates for building trust and fostering accountability within teams. Whether you're leading a small team or a large organization, this book provides the concrete tools needed to create a more engaged, purposeful, and high-performing workplace.'

—**Michael Wade,** Author and Professor at IMD, Lausanne; Director of the TONOMUS Global Center for Digital and AI Transformation

'Gaëlle Devins' new book brings a unique dimension to the art of leadership by bringing People, Performance and Purpose together. Her new framework FLOW@WORK is the outcome of these 3Ps process and a transformative guide for your own personal strategic advantage. Aimed primarily but not uniquely at practitioners, this book will improve the impact of your leadership style, increase your team productivity, and transform the ethos of your organization.'

—**Dr. Dominique Turpin,** Emeritus Professor, former Dean & President of IMD (Switzerland/Singapore)

'*Flow Leadership: The Power of the 3Ps* is an essential guide for leaders who want to create workplaces where people truly thrive. With over 23 years of leadership experience across various industries, Gaëlle Devins blends *People, Purpose and Performance* into a practical framework for fostering well-being alongside success. This book is particularly valuable for leaders looking to connect with the values of the emerging Gen Z workforce, emphasising the importance of aligning organisational goals with personal fulfilment. Gaëlle's deep insights and commitment to meaningful change make this book a powerful tool for transforming workplaces into spaces of care and growth.'

—**Jay Richards**
CEO, Imagen Insights

'FLOW@WORK masterfully captures the evolving expectations of today's workforce, particularly young professionals, who yearn for a leadership style that prioritises a holistic approach encompassing performance, people development, and a shared sense of purpose. Gaëlle´s practical and accessible guidance empowers leaders at all levels to cultivate a more fulfilling and impactful work environment. Her genuine passion shines through, making the journey towards building a stronger team and a more positive culture both inspiring and achievable.'

—**Andrea Gerosa**
Founder at Think Young

'Gaëlle Devins is one of the most creative and, at the same time, practical thinkers I have ever met. Her ability to perceive the complex and distill it to concepts and language that are digestible and comprehensive is unique amongst many people I have met in my life. Her work here is no different and offers new perspectives on existing ideas. And this is where Gaëlle excels. She can take the obscure and explain it in laymens' terms without condescension. I congratulate her on her latest work and hope that one day she will finally see the light, abandon her literary career, and come and help me lead my company to greatness.'

—**Andrew Farkas,** Chairman & CEO, Island Capital Group and Graduate Chairman, Hasty Pudding Institute of 1770, Harvard University

'Gaëlle Devins' *Flow Leadership* brilliantly highlights the transformative power of putting people first, offering a blueprint for creating workplaces where individuals thrive and companies excel. This book is an inspiring call to action for leaders who recognize that empowered and engaged people lead to extraordinary outcomes.'

—**Hubert Joly,** Former Best Buy CEO, Senior Lecturer at Harvard Business School, Best-Selling Author, *The Heart of Business*

'The world needs more fearless female leaders like Gaëlle Devins – trailblazers who don't just talk about change, but make it happen. For over a decade, Gaëlle has brought heart, empathy, and emotional intelligence into the boardrooms of high-end luxury brands, proving that leadership isn't just about strategy – it's about people. Her bottom-up approach is rewriting the leadership playbook, creating real impact where it matters most.

The Flow Leadership Method isn't just a book – it's a movement. Gaëlle is redefining what it means to lead with purpose, authenticity, and impact. If you're ready to step up, inspire, and drive real change, this is the leadership guide you've been waiting for.'

—**Shelley Zalis,** Founder and CEO, The Female Quotient

FLOW
Leadership

GAELLE DEVINS

FLOW Leadership

UNLEASH THE **POWER** OF **PEOPLE, PURPOSE,** AND **PERFORMANCE**

WILEY

This edition first published 2025

Registered Offices
John Wiley & Sons, Inc., 111 River Street, Hoboken, NJ 07030, USA
John Wiley & Sons Ltd, New Era House, 8 Oldlands Way, Bognor Regis, West Sussex, PO22 9NQ, UK

For details of our global editorial offices, customer services, and more information about Wiley products visit us at www.wiley.com.

The manufacturer's authorized representative according to the EU General Product Safety Regulation is Wiley-VCH GmbH, Boschstr. 12, 69469 Weinheim, Germany, e-mail: Product_Safety@wiley.com.

Wiley also publishes its books in a variety of electronic formats and by print-on-demand. Some content that appears in standard print versions of this book may not be available in other formats.

Library of Congress Cataloging-in-Publication Data is Available:

ISBN 9781394344864 (Cloth)
ISBN 9781394344871 (ePub)
ISBN 9781394344888 (ePDF)

Cover Design: Wiley
Cover Image: © VYACHESLAV KRAVTSOV/stock.adobe.com
Author Photo: Courtesy of Gaëlle Devins

Set in Sabon LT Std 13/16pt by Straive, Chennai, India.
Printed and bound by CPI Group (UK) Ltd, Croydon, CR0 4YY
C9781394344864_200525

The manufacturer's authorized representative according to the EU General Product Safety Regulation is Wiley-VCH GmbH, Boschstr. 12, 69469 Weinheim, Germany, e-mail: Product_Safety@wiley.com.

To all who dare to plant the seeds of change – leaders and beginners alike – may you find the rhythm of FLOW@WORK that transforms work into purpose, ignites hearts into action and turns every challenge into opportunity. This is your quest, and together, we shape a future where work becomes one of our greatest masterpieces.

Contents

Foreword

In leadership, as in watchmaking, precision and purpose are essential. Achieving sustainable growth requires more than just hitting targets – it demands a clear focus on creating long-term value for all relevant stakeholders, from shareholders to clients, through employees and local communities and of course for our planet. This book provides a pragmatic and insightful guide for leaders who aim to strike that balance, offering a framework rooted in principles that drive enduring success.

Sustainability is a principle that goes beyond environmental impact. It is about creating products or services, processes and cultures that endure – delivering results today while ensuring relevance and strength for the future. At Breitling, I've always prioritized this dual focus. Through disciplined execution and a clear vision, we have strengthened our legacy, built trust with our customers and driven long-term growth that stands the test of time.

I have had the privilege of knowing Gaëlle Devins for over 13 years and hiring her twice at two of the companies I have led. Now, as a Member of the Executive Board at Breitling, she continues to prove why she is one of the really effective leaders I have ever worked with. Everywhere she has been placed, she has turned around performance and set new benchmarks of excellence – not through shortcuts or quick fixes but by fundamentally shifting the approach to performance. Her strategy is always clear: prioritize colleagues and associates, both internally and externally. She creates environments where teams excel, and customers feel truly valued.

What sets Gaëlle apart is the balance she strikes. Yes, she is a commercial performance booster – driven, ambitious and results-focused. But she is also one of the most caring individuals I know, guided by strong values of fairness and trust. It is this rare combination of sharp business acumen and a heart big enough to care deeply for people that makes her approach so effective and transformational.

This book introduces the concept of *flow leadership*, a practical framework for creating environments where people can perform at their best while staying aligned with a shared purpose and delivering meaningful results. It recognizes that leadership is not just about managing tasks – it is about fostering a culture where teams thrive and businesses achieve sustainable excellence.

Putting people at the centre is not just a feel-good idea; it is a strategic imperative. A business thrives when its teams thrive. As a leader, it is your responsibility to ensure your people have the tools, clarity and support they need to succeed. When you invest in the growth and well-being of your team, you unlock their full potential – and in turn, the potential of your organization.

The concept of FLOW@WORK, as outlined in this book, takes this idea further by showing how leaders can cultivate optimal performance and engagement. It is not about chasing quick wins but about building sustainable systems that deliver consistent results over time.

At Breitling, we recognize the importance of balancing the 3Ps – *People, Purpose* and *Performance*. As we continue our journey, we have embraced *flow leadership* as part of our approach to driving meaningful change. Supporting the launch of this book by our chief customer officer is just one example of how we are aligning ourselves with these principles. By fostering an environment where teams can operate in their flow, we are not only ensuring success for today but also paving the way for the future.

Leadership is ultimately about balance – between purpose and performance, between short-term goals and long-term impact, and between empowering people and driving outcomes. This book offers practical strategies for achieving that balance, bridging the gap between bottom-line growth and embedding sustainable practices and management into the heart of your organization.

We know that the world is changing, and as a company committed to innovation, sustainability and excellence, we are determined to lead by example. *Flow leadership* is not just an idea – it is an actionable mindset that reflects the kind of organization we should aim for, one where every individual thrives, and every opportunity for greatness is seized.

Time and people are two of the most valuable resources we have as leaders. Use both wisely, invest in what truly matters, and lead with perceptiveness.

Georges Kern,
CEO Breitling

Why I Wrote This Book

In my life, I have faced many unexpected events often beyond my control, which caused chaos and uncertainty. During those times, my parents comforted me, telling me that things always happen for a reason. With time, I realized that my parents were right; there is always a reason for life's twists and turns. This is how I found resilience.

Yet my resilience was put to a severe test during my pregnancy with our twins. I was bedridden, my body ached all over, my mind was hazy and I was lonely. But strangely, I felt more alert and alive than ever before.

Life was forcing me to stop, giving me the chance to do something I had never found time or inspiration for before. Being bedridden allowed me to face my shadows. It became a moment of stillness and reflection; it transformed me and how I approached returning to the workplace.

At last, I understood that for most of my career, I have had two separate lives: the 'me at work', highly driven; and the 'me in my personal life', searching for meaning. Fearful of being judged by the corporate world, I feared displaying the part of me searching for purpose.

The birth of our twins changed all that. Carrying and giving life altered me; it was what ultimately made me decide to write this book. Writing felt both scary and exhilarating. It is in a way a coming out, sharing thoughts and ideas on how we can transform ourselves and the world around us – transforming how we work and how we lead.

Through decades of experience, I discovered that the heart of leadership beats in the genuine care for those you guide. You show up not only as a leader but as a mentor. It is about fostering a culture where happiness is not just a metric but a shared pursuit.

Whether in Geneva, London, Hong Kong or New York and regardless of the industry I was part of – FMCG, Fashion or Luxury – I saw how focusing on the well-being and happiness of my team translated into outstanding performance. When people feel valued and content, it sets the stage for incredible results.

This leadership style, which I now refer to as *flow leadership*, goes beyond the business metrics. It touches lives. It is in the commitment to see others as they are that the alchemy happens. Mentorship, a cornerstone of my leadership philosophy, personifies the transformative power of *flow leadership* from the bottom up. Without realizing it, finding *flow* guided me through my personal and professional challenges.

In addition, needless to mention that in the world of commerce, the principles of such leadership play an important role. When individuals feel recognized, they naturally channel that positive energy into client interactions. It creates an atmosphere of trust which translates into sales and customer loyalty.

Flow leadership becomes a catalyst for personal fulfilment. It allows individuals to express their true selves in the workplace. This, in turn, leads to higher job satisfaction, increased motivation and a willingness to make a difference. And all this leads an organization to becoming a community where individuals are partners (Figure 1).

Figure 1 FLOW@WORK: Cultivating Inner Growth and Fulfilment to Unlock Workplace Harmony

Flow leadership is a holistic transformation. It is a philosophy that drives not only success but also cultivates a thriving ecosystem.

The Power of the 3Ps

Successful organizations follow a common principle: they lead their people towards individual fulfilment and shared goals. This is the essence of *Flow Leadership* – a leadership style built on the power of the 3Ps – *People, Purpose* and *Performance.*

Flow Leadership embodies the ability to guide teams from *people* to *purpose* and *performance.* As a leader, ensuring that the 3Ps are in balance is essential. When one of the 3Ps dominates at the expense of the others, it creates an imbalance affecting the overall results.

But when you strike a balance between the 3Ps, you foster high-performance outcomes and FLOW@WORK. This is when your people feel at their best, are at their best and produce their best work.

The 3Ps Triangle of *Flow Leadership*

The First P: *People*; their well-being is the foundation of *flow leadership.*

The Second P: *Purpose*; it is about finding meaning at work. *Purpose* is the catalyst for experiencing FLOW@WORK and acts as the guiding force for the team.

The Third P: *Performance*; it is about matching the skills with challenges, leading to natural excellence.

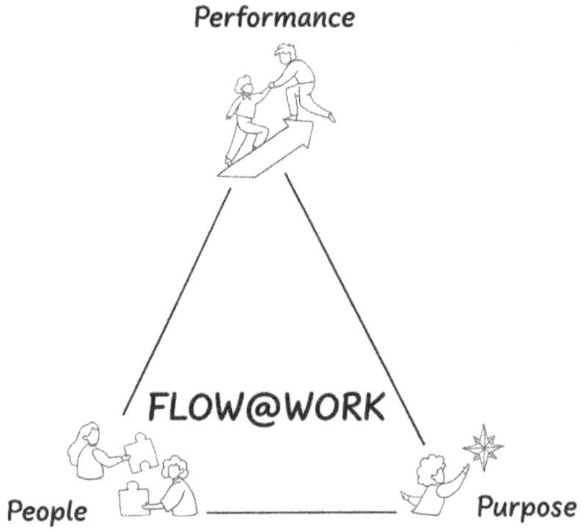

Figure 2 The 3Ps Triangle of *Flow Leadership*

FLOW@WORK is the outcome of the 3Ps process (Figure 2). This is what ensures a constant state of *flow*. Once found, *flow* transcends the individual level to the entire organization.

The graph below illustrates the direct link between *flow leadership* and *People, Purpose* and *Performance*, at individual, team and organizational levels (Figure 3).

The first layer, the base of the triangle, represents the focus on the individuals. It sets the foundation for a positive work environment and for personal growth and satisfaction.

When embraced by individuals, *flow leadership*, naturally leads to cohesive teams united by a common purpose. This second layer is demonstrated by teams becoming stronger units. This is when the collective outcome transcends individual contributions, creating a powerful force for success.

The final layer at the top of the triangle is where the results of *flow leadership* become evident. A culture rooted in authenticity and resilience attracts and retains top talent.

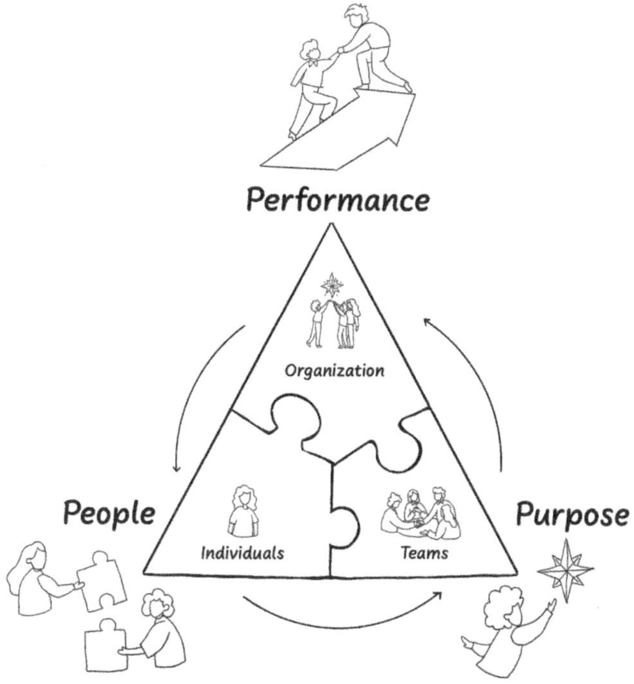

Figure 3 Connecting the 3Ps, *People, Purpose* and *Performance*: The Triangle of *Flow Leadership* in Organizations

Teams navigate challenges with adaptability, and the entire organization performs optimally.

Whether you are a seasoned leader or a newcomer, *flow leadership* is a transformative guide and your strategic advantage. When you, as a leader, shift your focus from performance to people and purpose, you will nurture the extraordinary.

It is time to change the workplace, putting its most valuable gem – PEOPLE – back in the centre. *Flow leadership* will revolutionize your team productivity and well-being and transform the ethos of your organization.

Embrace the principles within these pages and witness how it can and will transform your career and, ultimately, your life. Let us do it together.

Part I

People

1

Your Input Is Your Output

As leaders, our mission always starts with *people* and their well-being. It is what ensures a solid base for the entire structure to work. Focusing on the satisfaction of each and every individual is the foundation of *flow leadership*. When individuals are in *flow*, they form the bedrock of thriving organizations and cohesive teams. As this foundation strengthens, the natural progression is towards *purpose*.

Leaders who care and invest time in getting to know their team members create a place where people feel seen, heard, valued and motivated to give their best. Today, companies compete not on the services they provide but rather on the customer experiences (CXs) they deliver. If your team is happy, you will be happy and, above all, your clients will be happy.

Traditionally, companies have been heavily focused on branding, products and services. Only recently companies have started to realize the importance of client feedback and their customer needs. With this shift, the client became the centre of what truly matters, and CX became a company's best competitive edge. An unrivalled CX will deliver improved client loyalty, increased market share and revenues.

Customer experience is about changing your client engagement approach and moving away from a transactional mindset. As a leader, you play an integral role in this business transformation. By applying the principles of CX on your people internally, you will inspire them to replicate it with their clients. Your people are the beating heart of your brand and organization. They are the engines. They are the ones propelling your company's mission to succeed. Yet, any engine, small or big, needs maintenance and care.

Your input is your output. In other words, what you put in, you get out. As a leader, if you treat your employees as your most important clients, you will unlock the best CX and create a memorable employee experience (EX).

Employee experience is your employee's relationship with your company. It is the sum of their touchpoints, encounters and experiences in the workplace. Employee experience is not about having better coffee in the break room (although who does not love a good cuppa?). It goes much deeper. Employee experience is everything your people do, learn, experience, see and observe at each stage of their employee life cycle. It is about how the company makes them feel from before their first working day up until they leave your care.

To improve your EX, assess your employee life cycle in the same way you would do for your external client journey. Start by mapping out the five phases that your employees will experience within your company: recruitment, onboarding, development, retention and exit (Figure 1.1).

For each phase, identify the pain points, assess metrics, identify trends, listen, close the gap and monitor. Listen to your people's honest feedback. Research and understand their satisfaction level. Identify the metrics to be considered. Discover the moments that matter to your employees by collecting regular feedback from across their life cycle. When feedback is collected, be mindful and remain aware. Is the information gathered serving the company or your people? Through this process, you will learn how to design your company's optimal employee journey.

As a leader, your first step should be to ensure that the fundamentals are in place. The basics need to be covered, to name a few: equal pay, transparent career paths, fairness, diversity, transparency, a healthy work environment,

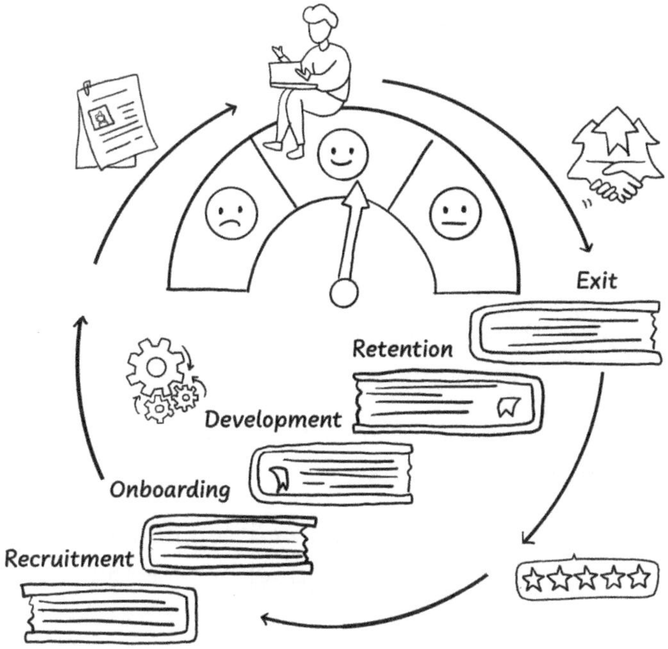

Figure 1.1 The Employee Experience Journey: Navigating the Five Phases of the Life Cycle

a clear mission and objectives. Be aware that the best internal customer relationship management (CRM) journeys will not be able to compensate for any voids in the above.

As a company you can have the best customer strategy, yet if you ignore your internal clients, a customer-centric framework will not succeed. To galvanize emotions towards external clients, your people should experience them first hand. Therefore, the formula for a successful client experience is very simple: your customer experience (CX) is your employee experience (EX) (Figure 1.2).

CX = EX. Your customer experience is your employee experience.

The employee experience should always be equal to the client experience. Experience is the common factor, and this is what unites the employees, the brand and the client. Approaching both disciplines – CX and EX – in a holistic and balanced manner is paramount.

Figure 1.2 CX = EX

Engaged employees are happy employees who are passionate about their jobs. They find meaning in what they do and therefore are motivated to go the extra mile to create a better CX. Today, companies have a wealth of data on CX and EX. Tomorrow, companies should create a new, emerging silo and stop operating CX and EX programmes separately.

A CX programme that does not include EX simply cannot reach its full potential. Creating a common measurement framework and correlating EX and CX data will uncover where the work needs to happen. This is what will help identify mutual dependencies and interconnected drivers.

Focusing too much on EX over CX will result in employees who lack customer service skills or do not deliver desired results. Conversely, prioritizing CX over EX might lead to high employee turnover and poor commercial performance.

But companies that balance both EX and CX understand their equal importance. This ensures employees are both satisfied and capable of delivering excellent customer service, ultimately leading to better business outcomes (Figure 1.3).

Figure 1.3 Balancing EX and CX: Aligning Employee and Customer Experiences for Business Success

Therefore, companies that recognize the significance of CX being equal to EX not only establish clear business goals but also provide a straightforward path for their employees to reach them. This understanding ensures that employees are aligned with the company's objectives and are equipped to contribute effectively to achieving these objectives.

Leaders are responsible for guiding their teams through this transformative journey, empowering their people to discover their FLOW@WORK. In doing so, leaders pave the way for their people to deliver unparalleled CXs, driving the success of the organization. Your role is not only pivotal but also immensely rewarding, as you witness your team members flourish and your company thrive. I urge you to embrace this challenge with confidence and dedication, knowing that your efforts will not only elevate your team but also leave a lasting impact on your customers and your business. Be the seed of change.

2

Dare to Care

Following the logic of CX = EX, in *flow leadership*, leaders understand that there is no commercial success without investing in the care for others. And this principle remains true regardless of whether your client is internal or external.

By being aware of your own needs, you can be even more present for the needs of your teams. Leaders often anticipate the needs of their teams. In such instances, it is paramount to seek validation through questions and to actively listen to the answers. Hear what is being said, decipher what is not being told, and witness what is being shown. Active listening is done with an open heart and genuine care and is focused on what is visible and what is not.

Some leaders believe that the traditional yearly performance cycle allows transparent discussions. Nothing could be further from the truth. Each employee will prepare for their performance meeting and remain cautious of what is said. After all, people want that promotion and salary increase. Why would they then potentially risk it by sharing honest feedback?

Alternatively, could you imagine if the employees were given a dedicated space to share their needs and ambitions and how safe it would make them feel? Feeling safe and trusting that the information disclosed would not impact their career. Now, imagine a time and space designed for that purpose instead of being linked to a performance review. What do you think would be the impact of such a process?

Your role as a leader is to foster such a culture, imprinted with emotions. Your ambition should be to create a safe place where your employees can fully show up as their authentic self to work every day.

Figure 2.1 Flow Leadership: Transitioning from Top-down Control to Inclusive, Nurturing Leadership

This is the ambition of *flow leadership* and the outcome of FLOW@WORK. It is about making your people feel at their best, be at their best, and produce their best work. It is about transitioning from a vertical, top-down type of leadership to a transversal, embracing and nurturing type of leadership (Figure 2.1).

It is about you as a leader daring to care for your *people*. Put your people's needs first, and your company's success will follow. It is and will always be about the *people*.

May the following principles provide you with fresh inspiration on how to *dare to care* for your *people*, the first 'P' of *flow leadership*.

3

Ask the Right Questions

Let's Talk about Needs

A leader's role should be about getting to know their people and understanding their needs. This is how leaders can start focusing on the first 'P', *people*, and their well-being. Asking the right questions will enable you to receive relevant information. This is powerful knowledge for a leader. This is your key to make informed leadership decisions and enhance your teams' performances.

The following personal story from a global company town hall illustrates the impact of triggering change through asking the right questions, fostering empathy and promoting collaborative leadership.

It was a bustling management and leadership conference hosted by one of the leading luxury companies I had the privilege of working for. Leaders and executives from various corners of the globe gathered in a large auditorium, brimming with energy and anticipation. The atmosphere was charged with the buzz of discussions and the hum of anticipation.

As I stepped onto the stage, I had that all familiar feeling of my heart racing and my hands sweating with nervousness. While I feel comfortable presenting when on stage, the walk up there had me on edge. Luckily, as soon as I locked eyes with the audience, I felt a deep sense of care for each person in the room. It was this genuine concern and connection that fuelled my determination to break away from the traditional mould of front-stage presentations. Instead of launching into a traditional top-down speech, I chose a different approach. 'Let us take a moment', I began, 'to reflect on our needs – not just as leaders in this company but as individuals striving for growth and fulfilment'.

The initial reaction was a mix of curiosity and scepticism. This was not the usual business rhetoric they were accustomed to. However, with a warm smile and gentle urging, I encouraged everyone to grab a pen and paper and engage in introspection.

As the room filled with the sound of pens scratching against paper, I could sense a shift in the atmosphere. It was no longer just about business metrics and strategies; it was about personal aspirations, values and the essence of leadership.

Joined by two members of my team, we shared our direct-to-consumer vision. I was not looking to achieve a polished solo performance; I wanted a collaborative sharing of insights and ideas.

The impact was most profound among the new leaders – the fresh faces eager to make their mark. They were inspired by the emphasis on empathy, teamwork and genuine care for the *people*. It sparked a realization that leadership is not just about authority but about creating a supportive and inclusive environment for all.

This concept was illustrated by bringing two of my team members on stage – *theory in action*. This action represented more than just symbolic inclusion; it was about *walking the talk* and demonstrating our commitment to fostering a supportive and growth-oriented environment. By having them on stage, we showcased first hand the importance of caring for the *people* and empowering them to succeed. This approach exemplified the idea that leadership is not just about speaking or theorizing but about taking concrete steps to implement positive change and lead by example.

In that room, amidst the backdrop of a global business meeting, a subtle yet powerful transformation had taken place. Minds were opened, perspectives shifted, and a new era of leadership – one grounded in empathy and collaboration – could start emerging. It was *flow leadership* in the making.

The day I shared my thoughts and insights during that global company town hall became a turning point, as it became the catalyst for change across local teams. The feedback I received from these teams in various markets was enlightening; their leaders had returned with a renewed perspective on team care and appreciation. It was heartening to witness how this meeting had sparked a wave of positivity and gratitude.

Once back home, many leaders took proactive steps to celebrate their teams' achievements, organizing special gatherings and recognition events. Others made the conscious efforts to spend time and ask questions to their teams. These gestures were not just about acknowledging milestones; they were about expressing genuine appreciation for the hard work and dedication shown by each team member.

What truly struck me was the ripple effect of my message. It was not just about words spoken in a town hall; it was about inspiring action and meaningful change. This was evident when a senior member, highly respected within the company, took the time to write personalized thank-you notes after a major project. These handwritten notes were not just tokens; they were sincere expressions of gratitude that resonated deeply with the teams involved.

Drawing from real-life experiences like the one shared above, my book emphasizes the importance of *theory in action* and provides practical exercises to empower leaders in fostering a culture of empathy, collaboration and growth within their teams and organizations.

While most of the feedback was positive, it did not win the hearts of all. And that is fine. Remember, you are not always going to get everyone. You might have been a sceptic in that room; you might still be. However, what if I were to tell you that even implementing a fraction – say 10% or 20% – of these ideas can significantly impact workplace dynamics and, hence, overall performance? Those ideas could lead to better retention of top talent, addressing a common reason for their departure: feeling undervalued and uncared for in the workplace.

With these principles in mind, I invite you to engage in the following exercise. Let us practise asking the right questions. Get a pen and paper or open the note on your mobile device. This exercise helps you recognize your own needs and understand what your team will experience when you do this exercise with them.

Exercise: Practise the Art of Asking the Right Question

Please reflect on this first question:

> *What are your needs to feel at your best, be at your best and produce your best work?*

Apart from the obvious responses, let us focus solely on you and be more specific.

> *What are your needs at work?*
> *What do you need to feel happy at work?*
> *What do you need to be successful at work?*

Jot down your initial thoughts. When you are prepared, we will proceed to the next question.

When was the last time that you sat down and thought about your needs?

Try to remember. If you cannot, maybe this is something that you should start reflecting a bit more on. If you have gone as far as to have thought about your needs, ask yourself:

When was the last time you did something about your needs?
What actions did you take?

Now that you have considered your needs, think about the needs of your people, individually and as teams.

What are the needs of your team, individually and collectively?
What are their needs to feel at their best, be at their best and produce their best work?

If you do not lead a team, think about the needs of your colleagues or your peers. The logic remains the same.

Let us go one step further.

Do you know their triggers?
Do you know their emotional keys?

Emotional keys are triggers. These are the small things that make our hearts race with excitement and bring us happiness.

What are their dreams?
Do you know their career aspirations?

What do they need to feel fulfilled and on the path to reaching optimal performance when at work?
What makes each one of them so special?
What are their hidden talents, strengths and motivations?
Do you know what they want, need and value right now?
What are their biggest concerns and challenges?
What type of support will make their lives easier and happier more in the flow?

Explore beyond these questions and focus on building meaningful relationships with your people. This is how you will cultivate long-term loyalty.

Think of how and when to ask these questions. Prompt them during a workshop or a meeting. Choosing your moments when and how to raise those questions is as important as choosing the right questions.

That process should be about your people, not about you. Be clear on your intentions. What is it that you are seeking: the truth or a sugar-coated version of the truth?

The choice is yours. One path will lead your organization towards change; the other route will please your ego and maintain the status quo.

Establishing trust within a team is crucial for receiving honest answers and fostering a positive work environment. This trust is built through genuine connections, which can be achieved by getting to know your teams on a personal level and experiencing their daily work life first hand. This approach resonates strongly with my experience in retail management, where I found that immersing myself in the daily activities of our teams led to significant improvements in performance and morale.

During my time in retail management in North America, I thrived on the excitement of the job: the travel, the energy and the interactions with new staff and clients in our boutiques. I realized that being away from my office was the best way to understand the unique needs and challenges faced by our teams and clients.

By spending time with my teams in the field and experiencing their work environment first hand, I gained valuable insights into their daily routines, pain points and aspirations. This hands-on approach allowed me to empathize with their concerns and understand their perspectives more deeply. As a result, I became more comfortable asking questions and addressing issues head-on, which in turn helped me earn their trust and respect.

This deeper level of connection and trust was instrumental in turning around the performance of our retail team in North America. By actively listening to their feedback, implementing targeted improvements based on their input and fostering a culture of open communication and collaboration, we were able to boost morale, increase productivity and achieve significant growth in sales and customer satisfaction metrics. This experience reinforced my belief in the power of building strong relationships and understanding the needs of your teams to drive positive outcomes in any organizational setting.

If this resonates with you, collect in a notebook all the questions that have inspired you over the years. Each time you come across a new question, add it to your list. Take time to review those questions regularly. Make them part of your interaction with your teams. At first, it may be difficult to implement it. Maybe it will be worth adding gentle reminders to your calendar. And like anything in life, the more you practise the art of asking the right questions, the more it will become an integral part of your leadership style.

Figure 3.1 Offer a Lifeline Through Open Dialogue Before Your People Start to Sink

Empowering your team through open dialogue starts with making them feel acknowledged and heard (Figure 3.1). Each answer they provide gives you valuable insights and pointers, which are crucial for effective leadership.

4

Equip Your *People* for Success

When you understand your *people* better, empowered with the fresh knowledge of what their needs are, you can look at your business with a holistic view. Companies and leaders often focus their time looking at the building blocks required to reach their commercial objectives. Often, the same exercise is forgotten on the *people* front.

Sadly, this creates an imbalance. The speed of development and growth becomes unsustainable for the *people*. Therefore, correlating the needs of your teams with the needs of your business is what will enable you as a leader to put in place the building blocks on the *people* front.

To anticipate the impact on your people, ask yourself the following question:

How will you equip your teams, individually and collectively, to achieve the objectives?

To be successful as a leader, you need to set your people up for success. So think for a moment about each one of them.

What are their strengths?
What are their areas for development?

From there, partner with the right department to develop accurate training plans. Spend time looking into the type of support your people will need. That is when and how you can show up for your teams.

The first exercise could be about identifying and developing the strengths of your people. Ask each team member to list out their strengths, discuss and validate them during an open team conversation. Or you can conduct a strength assessment questionnaire. There are many on the market.

This will help you identify your people's unique talents and strengths.

Once this is done, ask each of your team members to share their top strengths with the rest of the team. This will help create a culture of appreciation and understanding. Then, discuss openly how each team member can leverage their strengths in their current role and explore opportunities for aligning tasks with their unique abilities. While this should not become a cherry-picking exercise, it can help shuffle a few things around to raise your teams' efficiencies.

To wrap up this exercise, encourage each team member to create a personal development plan focused on enhancing their strengths and acquiring new skills. This process often helps you better understand who in your team is vested in your company's success or not.

Beyond this traditional approach, try to be creative in how to equip your people. One notion that I introduced in one of my previous roles is the concept of 'edutainment': education and entertainment (Figure 4.1). When *edutainment*

Figure 4.1 Edutainment: Transforming Learning Through Engaging Experiences

is organized around experiences, employees become active participants in the learning process.

It helps them make meaning of these experiences. The goal is not just to give out information and hope it sticks. Instead, the aim is to create engaging training sessions tailored to your business needs. Through these experiences, participants actively engage with the material, making it more likely to stick. They will remember it better because they have lived it, not just heard about it. This approach ensures that the training is not only informative but also memorable and effective.

In addition, your objective should be to ensure that 'training' is seen as an enabler of performance. Often, training or development workshops are seen as an afterthought. People sign up with good intentions. However, when other business needs come up or other projects became priorities, these sessions become abandoned. Other times, the trainings offered are not in sync with their current needs. That is why it is crucial to match the training offer to the current business and personal development needs. This is a great step towards repositioning training overall. The key is to make this discipline *relevant*.

The perception and image of your training department are critical. Your company needs to see it as an enabler of success and performance. And you, as a leader, can make it a 'hot' topic. Training is essential for improving your team's performance. It gives them the confidence and knowledge they need to succeed. With proper training, your teams will tackle challenges and excel in their roles, driving success for your organization.

In one of my previous roles, together with my team, we repositioned and changed the name of our 'training department' to 'team performance training department'. The word 'performance' brought this department to another level.

It was all about making our story credible and showing the impact our discipline has on the bottom line. By using numbers, we were able to commercialize the impact of training. It did the trick. At last, others could see the added value of partnering with our department, later known as the SWAT team.

Beyond repositioning our image and building our credibility through performance, we built *learning journeys*, using the logic of a 'coloured belts' system. The symbolism of the coloured belt system was to illustrate the stops required along the way – similar to its use in martial arts, where one would be required to demonstrate focus, dedication and discipline. Only those who practise will succeed. Only those who have patience and resilience will pursue the road to self-mastery.

On this principle, Jigoro, a well-regarded teacher in Japan in the late 1800s, created judo from his study of jujitsu. He began awarding his students the rank of *shodan*, literally 'beginning degree'. The ranking then became a form to recognize the student's level of mastery of the discipline and reward the commitment and achievement. Now, the coloured belt system is adopted by many martial art disciplines. The colours of martial arts belts denote the student's development, skills and experience in a specific area.

The mastery of the discipline is a journey. It all starts from the mastery of the basics. At each level, the knowledge is tested to confirm it has been assimilated. This allows the student to create a solid base and to develop the strengths in a more sustainable way. This is what inspired us to design *learning journeys*.

To have the best output, there is a need to understand who those trainings are designed for. Now, more than ever, time is scarce, and people find it increasingly difficult to sit and pay attention for long periods of time. Using empathy to enhance and humanize digital learning is how a company illustrates its people-centric mastery. Over the years, I have discovered that the most effective approach for my teams is to offer blended learning journeys. By combining online, offline and experiential training methods, we break the monotony and create more engaging learning experiences. This variety not only keeps participants interested but also helps them retain information better.

As a leader, achieving your company's objectives requires more than just preparing your people for success. It is more than just equipping them with skills and knowledge. Your role is to ignite their passion and motivation. Provide them with the tools, support and encouragement they need to thrive. Because fuelled employees are the key to driving organizational success.

5

Coach to Empower

Asking the right questions, edutainment and blended learning journeys are great ways to understand and equip your teams. Let us take it one step further. Coach to empower. This will provide your people with a certain degree of autonomy, control and decision-making opportunities and will ultimately enable them to grow even more.

However, there is a fine balance to maintain in terms of coaching and support. If you are too present, your people will not feel empowered to make decisions. As a result, they will heavily rely on you. As a leader, your role is to explain openly what the process is to get to a decision. It is also about showing how to deal with the consequences of a good or not-so-good decision.

There is always an element of risk in each decision a leader takes. And that is fine. What is important, though, is to show how to readjust and learn from any lessons. Encourage your people to try, and try again, until success comes. Put in place a safety net to promote a growth mindset. Remember, there are no failures. There are only learning moments. Instead of telling your employees how it is done, show them. When such a strategy is deployed properly, it should result in heightened productivity and a better work–life quality for you and your people.

Empowering your people involves expanding their horizons beyond the familiar. It means encouraging them to step out of their comfort zones and embrace new challenges. This growth mindset is essential for personal and professional development. As they venture into new territories, their roles become more fulfilling, and their confidence grows.

With each new challenge mastered – think Judo-style belts – your team members gain valuable experience and insight. They become more adept at navigating complex situations and finding innovative solutions. This boosts their confidence and energizes them to tackle even more ambitious goals.

As your people find their stride, they strike a balance between their skills and the challenges they face. This state of *flow* enables them to perform at their best, leveraging their experience, judgement, and creativity to excel in their roles. They become less reliant on strict rules and procedures, instead relying on their own intuition and expertise to drive results.

Empowered employees are the driving force of a successful organization. They are highly engaged, dedicated and committed to achieving the company's goals. With a sense of ownership and autonomy, they work harder and more efficiently to drive results.

Additionally, empowered employees tend to be more loyal to the company, as they feel valued and appreciated for their contributions. With empowerment and a transparent workplace culture, employees clearly see the impact of their work. This visibility and appreciation are great motivators.

The key to unlocking the full potential of empowerment lies in effective communication. It is crucial to clearly communicate the intent to empower employees throughout the organization. By sharing the organization's goals and objectives, employees understand how their individual efforts contribute to the overall success of the company. This alignment fosters a sense of unity and purpose among team members, driving them towards common objectives.

When employees are empowered and aligned with the organization's mission, they work cohesively towards shared goals, with a *purpose* in mind. This creates a harmonious work environment where tasks are executed with precision and efficiency. As a result, the organization becomes more agile and responsive to challenges, with empowered employees acting as proactive problem-solvers.

Ultimately, it all boils down to upskilling your people and fostering their managerial capabilities. While some leaders may be born with the gift of knowing how to coach and manage, the reality is that everyone needs to be given the means to reach their objectives. It is easy to tell employees what decisions they can or cannot make, but it will not be sufficient.

Empowerment requires leaders to give their employees the tools – the skills and the right level of guidance; they need to make high-quality decisions. And let us be honest; this process is time-consuming.

Quality coaching can be exhausting. Preparing employees to take on decision-making roles requires significant upfront investment in managerial coaching. Both leaders and employees need time to adjust to these new relationships.

This adjustment process temporarily slows down decision-making and adds to the workload of leaders who are coaching. Therefore, it is only natural to feel tempted to step back in and take over when things get challenging. However, giving in to this temptation will not help. It will instead promote co-dependency and short-term thinking.

The key is to resist the temptation, work through the challenges and trust that your coaching efforts will yield positive results in the long run (Figure 5.1). Trust me, it will. In time, your people will become more independent and give back the time you initially invested in coaching them.

As a leader, I found myself spending more time coaching and developing my team than on traditional tasks, like creating PowerPoint presentations. Initially, this shift in focus felt like I was cheating somehow – as if I was not doing 'real work'. It took me a while to realize that this

Figure 5.1 Keep Your Eyes on the Peak: Navigate the Path and Keep Moving Forward

is the essence of leadership – investing time and energy in people and their development. For me personally, what helped me find peace with this was my partner Chance's insightful perspective. He taught me that leadership is not about shouldering all the work alone; it is about adopting a helicopter view and strategically coaching the team towards collective success.

While I am here many years later, reflecting on this time invested in helping team members, there was a period when I struggled with feelings of guilt for not being 'productive' in the traditional sense. However, as I delved deeper into coaching and mentoring, team development initiatives, and fostering a culture of growth through feedback on the job, I began to understand the true essence of leadership. It is not about ticking off tasks on a checklist but about empowering and enabling others to reach their full potential to collectively meet business ambitions.

One moment stands out particularly to me in my journey. I was working closely with a team member who was struggling with self-confidence. He always self-doubted and would not bring his ideas to the forefront in a group setting. He had such potential, but the fear of what other people thought, the fear of being judged, paralysed him into not participating. Through mentoring and coaching sessions, I watched him blossom and take on new challenges with newfound courage. Seeing his growth and success was incredibly fulfilling; it reinforced my belief in the power of investing in *people*.

This experience taught me that leadership is about showing up for the *people* you lead. It is about creating an environment where everyone can thrive and contribute their best work. Instead of feeling guilty about focusing on coaching and development, I learned to embrace it as my unique strength as a leader.

And along the way, I discovered that challenging myself outside of my comfort zone and seeking mentorship were crucial steps in my own journey of growth and development. Initially, I was hesitant to step outside my familiar tasks and routines, fearing failure or the unknown. However, I realized that true growth happens when we push ourselves beyond what is comfortable.

Seeking mentorship played a pivotal role in this journey. I was fortunate to have mentors who guided me, shared their experiences and encouraged me to explore new approaches to leadership. They helped me navigate challenges, gain fresh perspectives and develop my own leadership style.

I want to stress the importance here of continuous learning and adaptation. Challenging situations forced me to learn and adapt quickly, whether it was learning new coaching techniques, embracing innovative leadership strategies or honing my communication skills.

One memorable experience involved leading a cross-functional team for a complex project. Directing a team who did not view me as their leader was a daunting task. Initially, they did not see the need for the initiative. Moreover, as my goals were not aligned with their KPIs, there was a lot of push-backs. There was even some active hostility from members of the team who felt their function should be leading these types of projects.

And to overcome this challenging situation, I used the 3P's *flow leadership* triangle. First, I focused on *people* and their needs. Everyone in that team wanted leadership roles and exposure to board members. Once this point was understood, I gave them that opportunity, which gained their engagement.

Next, I focused on *purpose* and aligned their individual purposes with the taskforce's purpose. Their goals were growth and career progression, while the taskforce aimed to break silos. I showed them how working together in a transversal manner could benefit both their careers and the organization.

For *performance*, we assessed each team's strengths. We assigned leadership based on natural skills and established agreed-upon KPIs. This consolidated our commercial ambition.

Finally, I adjusted my leadership style. Instead of leading, I coordinated and highlighted their strengths, like a maestro. This approach worked, demonstrating *flow leadership* in action.

By challenging myself to step into unfamiliar territory, and with the support of my mentor whom I used as a sounding board, I grew tremendously as a leader. The project's success not only boosted my confidence but also reinforced the value of embracing challenges and learning from them.

In sharing this story, I aim to inspire others to step outside their comfort zones, seek mentorship and embrace challenges as opportunities for growth. Leadership is not just about what we know; it is also about our willingness to learn, adapt and evolve continuously.

Coaching is not only about empowering others but also about being open to receive coaching for our own empowerment, enabling us to lead more effectively and foster a culture of growth and development within our teams.

6

Establish Firm Boundaries

Create a Healthy Work Environment

Getting to know your team and guiding them will strengthen your connection with them more than ever. As you continue your journey in *flow leadership*, let us revisit when you first started. By daring to care, a stronger bond should have begun to form. Setting boundaries will then help you stay focused on your goals and on the right path.

Boundaries are essential for a team to function effectively. As a leader, you can be generous and compassionate while maintaining clear boundaries. You can offer support, listen empathetically and have an open heart yet still establish firm boundaries.

Having well-defined boundaries does not diminish your accessibility; rather, it ensures that your needs and boundaries are known, respected and integrated into your leadership style. This clarity enables others to understand how to interact with you effectively while still feeling supported and valued. Defined boundaries define a person. You can be highly successful in your career, with well-defined boundaries, and still be sought after for advice.

As you invest more time in your people, it becomes increasingly important to communicate and establish your own boundaries.

> *As a leader, have you ever communicated your boundaries to your team?*
> *Do you know what your own boundaries are?*
> *Have you taken the time to understand the boundaries of your team members?*
> *And if you're aware of their boundaries, are they respected by each party?*

Figure 6.1 Defining Boundaries: Creating a Manifesto for Team Harmony

Take a moment to reflect on these questions. And as a next step, try to establish your boundaries as a leader and become clear about the ones of your teams, individually and collectively (Figure 6.1). Once these are clearly set and established, everyone in your team should be aware of each other's boundaries. A symbolic way for everyone to respect each other's boundaries is to sign a 'boundary manifesto'. A 'boundary manifesto' is a set of guidelines that individuals or teams establish to define and maintain healthy boundaries.

This manifesto outlines specific rules, expectations and limits regarding personal space, time, emotions, communication and relationships. It serves as a declaration of one's boundaries and the team's boundaries, preferences and needs, helping to create clarity and mutual understanding in interactions with others. A 'boundary manifesto' promotes self-care, respect and balanced relationships by establishing clear guidelines for healthy and respectful interactions. This can be done formally or informally and will ensure that boundaries are not only known and understood but 'enforced'.

During the process of establishing boundaries, you will hesitate and even refrain from stating your own needs and boundaries. Please do not. Start with what could be the most obvious. Pick a boundary that will serve you and your people. Choose a hot topic like, for example, 'work–life balance', as this is what your people often try to achieve.

Maybe express how your intention is to respect holidays and after working hours. Tell your people that you will refrain from sending emails during out of office hours. I picked this boundary as an example because too many times leaders always prioritize the business needs.

Reflecting earlier on in my career, I often used to prioritize the business above my own needs, boundaries and people. In fact, I must have been an absolute nightmare for my teams. Single and a workaholic. What a combo! Now, years later, I understand that even if was not asking them to follow suit, simply by working late at nights or on weekends, I was sending the wrong signals. Not only that, but it was also stressful for my teams because they would see the emails coming through during their time off. It took for me to become a mother of twins to understand the importance of boundaries. I was no longer able to work in the same way. I needed to establish a healthier way of working, with firm boundaries in place, between time off and time at work.

Starting with the 'work–life' boundary will make your people realize that you are expecting them to have boundaries in their life too. It will show your people you care enough for them and expect them to switch off during their time off. This will also reassure your people that performance is not about how long and hard you work; it is about the value you add to the business.

If this boundary does not resonate, pick another one or a few others. You will, as the leader, need to initiate the process. Speak your truth. Be authentic. Whatever your boundaries are, remember, share them openly. By clearly stating your needs and setting boundaries for yourself, you will be setting an example for your team. Often, leaders hesitate to share their boundaries because they consider it too personal. But if you do not do it, your team will not either.

And your role as a flow leader is to inspire change and help your employees understand that boundaries are another lever to reach peak performance for all. Remember, your input is your output.

7

Bring Healing Strategies to Your Workplace

Healing strategies can sometimes be a taboo topic, yet as a flow leader you play a fundamental role in humanizing the workplace. We have seen so far your role in getting to know and understanding your people, equipping and coaching them for success, and establishing clear boundaries. There is, however, another dimension that as a leader is often overlooked: providing time and space to *heal*. Enable your people to *heal*. Introduce healing strategies in your workplace. Sounds crazy? Then, read on.

A couple of years ago, one of the articles I published on LinkedIn resonated deeply and moved many. It was titled 'Breaking the Taboo: A Transparent Discussion about Miscarriage and the Workplace'.

As a leader and someone who experienced the profound pain of miscarriages, I understand the challenges of navigating personal struggles while showing up for others in a professional capacity. My journey to motherhood was not conventional; I found my partner later in life, and the path to conception was filled with uncertainty and heartache.

The dream of starting a family was something I never gave up on, despite the setbacks. Each miscarriage felt like a crushing blow to my hopes and dreams. The emotional toll was immense, and there were moments when it was incredibly difficult to maintain composure and focus on my leadership role. How could I support and lead others when my own heart was shattered?

It was during these darkest moments that I realized the importance of breaking taboos and fostering healing discussions in the workplace. The stigma around miscarriage and fertility struggles often silences individuals who are quietly suffering. If there had been a safe space for open dialogue and support, perhaps my own healing journey would have been less lonely and isolating.

Writing this article was my way of sharing not just my personal story but also advocating for healing strategies in the workplace. We cannot separate our personal struggles from our professional lives entirely. Healing hearts, minds, and bodies should be part of the organizational culture, promoting empathy, understanding, and resilience among team members.

While the solutions to such profound challenges may not always be clear or straightforward, I remain hopeful that with compassion, awareness and supportive environments, we will create a workplace where everyone feels seen, heard and valued, regardless of the obstacles they may face outside of work.

Bringing to the surface topics that are considered taboo will point out latent needs that have not been yet addressed. Time to heal is essential. Whatever the pain, whether it be physical, mental or emotional, there is a time needed for recovery and healing. But if the topic is considered taboo, your people will most likely have to suffer alone. That is the opposite of what they need. If taboos were broken in the workplace, embarrassment would disappear, and stories could be shared.

An amazing thing happens when people share their situations. It creates empathy. Sharing stories may trigger the healing process for both the narrators and the listeners. That is why it is so important to feel like it is okay to talk about what has often been considered taboo in the workplace. Everyone should be comfortable with, or at least supportive of, this approach.

As a leader, one effective way to begin is by openly sharing your own journey of healing. While this might seem daunting, it sends a powerful message to your team.

It helps break the stigma surrounding difficult topics and makes conversations about them more comfortable.

By showing vulnerability, you demonstrate that healing from trauma and experiencing anxiety or fear is a normal part of being human. This openness encourages employees who may be struggling to join in such discussions, making them feel less isolated in their healing journey.

Think about it. Would not it be amazing if companies provided employees who suffered a trauma time to heal and recover? How much easier could the healing process be if a person suffering knew it was okay to share their stories? As a leader, imagine how your people would feel. That would make a huge difference. If you dare to care for your people, then why not create the tools needed and give them the space to heal?

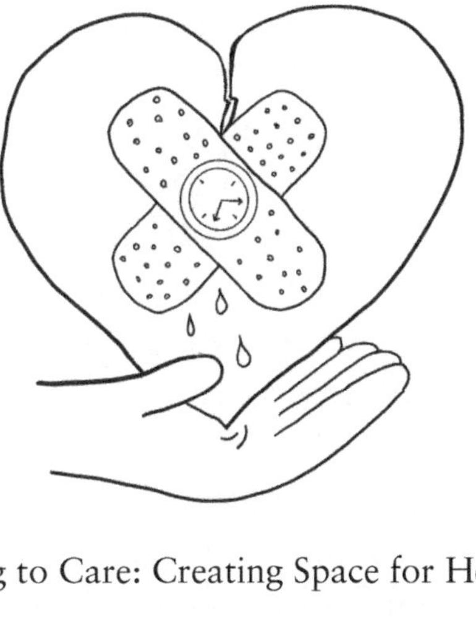

Figure 7.1 Daring to Care: Creating Space for Healing and Recovery

Your people will not perform unless they feel whole. And while your role is not the one of a therapist, your role is to give the time for your people to recover and heal (Figure 7.1). That is one of the most powerful things you can do as a leader who dares to care. And that is what an emotionally intelligent business would do.

Today, healing is a word that is being used more often in mainstream culture. Healing the nation, healing the people, healing the climate. It is a beautiful word and I have always struggled to understand why it is not used in the corporate setting. Healing will have a transformational effect on the people and the entire workplace.

Leaders often will offer sympathy and may feel sad for an employee who has experienced a trauma. But why not go beyond those feelings and act? Supporting an employee through the healing process creates an employee who is present and engaged when back at work.

If you give time for healing, what you receive is a workforce that is grateful and seeks to give back to the company that was there for them. By listening, showing up and being there, the business itself is acting humanely.

By putting actionable steps in place that help your employees better return to work, companies will see major benefits. When you respond to the human needs of your people, they recognize that. Employees snap back to being more productive and more honest. Communication goes from guarded to collaborative. Trust is earned, and your people will now be more motivated to give their best at work.

Returning employees deserve to be supported properly. Unfortunately, many workplaces lack a clear transition plan, especially in today's hybrid workplace. And unfortunately, without this plan, the return can be sources of stress rather than an opportunity for growth.

Supporting and helping your people through this time do not need to be the business disruption it can sometimes be seen as. It can be much more productive through authentic support and honesty. It can be better to be realistic. This is where honest conversations will help to minimize the stress and uncertainty. In challenging or transitional times, showing up for employees can mean so much.

It is easy for business leaders to miss this sometimes. Being a leader is no small task. You can create a nurturing environment where employees who suffered any sorts of trauma can thrive. It is how you plant the seeds of change. This is a soft way to introduce the notion of 'healing strategies' and could be a great launch platform to explain what healing means for you, your people and your organization overall.

8

Reconsider Your Current Metrics and KPIs

As you discover what *flow leadership* is, I encourage you to take a moment and think about the following:

> *Until now, have you focused more on your team's well-being or yourself?*
> *Are you supporting your company by supporting your team, or are you maybe more focused on your own success?*
> *Do you demonstrate genuine care for your team members?*
> *What steps have you taken so far to show that you care about them?*
> *Is your concern for your team's performance driven by genuine care, or is it just about meeting the next targets?*

My bet is that until now, you thought you had your people's best interests at heart. And you probably did. But somehow the system took over. The constant pressure to deliver more with limited resources to save costs is exhausting and nerve-racking. Being a leader is hard, and it is even more difficult to show up on all fronts.

Often, business needs take priority and, even with the best intentions, your people's needs fall by the wayside. Not by lack of will, but rather by lack of time and conflicting priorities. I have been there. Many times. Juggling so many tasks at once that it felt like I could not breathe freely. I felt stretched and, in those circumstances, how could I give to my *people* when I was running around to meet all demands? I certainly felt like I did not have time or energy left to do this type of work. The energy left I had, I chose to put it on what mattered at the time: project delivery to meet ambitious timelines, commercial targets and any other business needs.

My turning point was my years in retail management. This is when I realized that the circle needed to be broken. A retail sales teams does not operate like we do in an office environment. Their day to day is so different, and I was able to connect more with my *people* when I was in the field. When I was away from my corporate desk, I finally understood how essential it is for *people* to feel that they matter. It is essential for *people* to be cared for and placed at the forefront of any business strategies. The time vested in making them feel that way was time saved down the line. There is no point in asking more of our *people* (I am guilty of this) if they are running on empty.

Now, let us imagine that you were to take some time as a team to reset and release the past. If there was a time-out to establish a healthier, new way of working, what do you think would happen? Let me tell you – pure magic.

And as a leader, you have the power to claim that time for yourself and your *people*. You can change the way we currently work and create a happier and healthier workplace. How? By implementing some of the ideas shared earlier, as well as by bringing new KPIs that are designed for the *people* and not the system. Dare to introduce metrics that will help you assess how your *people* are doing and feeling, as opposed to how they are performing.

In *flow leadership*, an essential metric is the 'flow level', assessable at both individual and team levels, as well as the 3Ps assessments. This topic will be covered in Part III of this book.

In addition to this, you can introduce traditional metrics revolving around the employee journey. As previously discussed, the correlation between customer experience (CX) and employee experience (EX) is significant. Much like customer journeys, your employee life cycle involves various touchpoints, including hiring, onboarding, training, coaching, performance improvement plans, recognition and promotion. It is crucial to actively assess, measure and analyse the experience across each of these touchpoints. By doing so, you can identify areas for improvement as an organization.

Another critical metric involves matching the challenge to skills based on strengths, which we will further explore in Part III of this book. This is tied to the third 'P', *performance*.

In prioritizing KPIs that serve the *people* rather than solely focusing on the system, leaders demonstrate a commitment to their team's well-being and growth. While the ultimate outcome may benefit the organization, the initial priority lies in ensuring that the needs and experiences of individuals are addressed and valued.

Figure 8.1 Rethinking KPIs: Shifting Focus from Systems to People

It is important to recognize that by prioritizing a people-centric KPI approach, leaders ultimately contribute to the overall success and performance of the organization. While some may argue that serving the people is, in essence, serving the system, it is crucial to acknowledge that the primary focus and benefits should be directed towards the individuals within the organization (Figure 8.1).

By nurturing a culture that prioritizes the well-being and development of the *people*, leaders lay the foundation for a thriving and high-performing workplace. In doing so, they foster a sense of trust, loyalty and commitment among team members, leading to increased productivity, innovation and success for the organization.

A great place to start is to implement surveys for all relevant touchpoints. Even better, replace your employee engagement survey with regular pulse surveys and open feedback platforms. Go as far as including your candidates' interviews, engagement surveys, ongoing performance conversations and, of course, your exit interviews. This will give you a real-time understanding of the issues your people face.

Instead of chasing a metric, remember to keep the focus on EX improvements and business results. And just in case you wondered, keeping your surveys anonymous will not serve a purpose. If, as a leader, you managed to successfully create a safe place at work, your people should not be concerned about how their feedback can affect their careers and relationships at work. The foundation of a strong team lies in trust. Anonymous feedback sends the wrong message. It means that the feedback culture was not implemented in your organization. It means that providing feedback is 'not safe'.

Look beyond your usual metrics. The only way to get enough information for improvements is to deeply analyse the various aspects of EX and not just overall scores. This was one of the main drivers for me to write about *flow leadership* and the power of the 3Ps. I wanted processes and tools that would give me a true reading on how my teams, individually and collectively, were doing. I wanted my people to feel good so that they could perform at their best and find their FLOW@WORK. Deep down, I knew, and witnessed it endlessly, that when a person is in *flow*, stronger performance always follows. This is my wish for you to experience it first-hand if this is not already the case for yourself and your *people*. May you and your *people* find your FLOW@WORK, individually and collectively.

9

Reflect on Your *Flow Leadership* Journey

Focusing on *people* will help you create a meaningful performant workplace. And in a way, it will bring you back to the basics of what leadership is supposed to be – a means to inspire and enable others. It is my hope that you embrace some of the ideas and principles shared in Part I of this book. Because I wish for you to feel and witness the impact it will have on your *people*, their well-being and overall performances.

As flow leaders, let us remember that the input is the output and that in daring to care for your people, you will foster positive emotions and build a lasting bond. By equipping and coaching your people, you will empower them to reach new heights. And by sharing your boundaries at work and introducing healing strategies, you will nurture trust by protecting their well-being. And when we, as leaders, genuinely show up for the people, we create a spark that ignites performance through *purpose*, the second 'P' in *flow leadership*.

Before moving on to Part II of this book, which is dedicated to *purpose*, I encourage you to take a moment to check in with yourself and ponder the below:

> *What could be a few new actions that you could take to dare to care for your people?*
> *Are you aware of your people's needs?*
> *If you are, this is fantastic! So how do you provide them the relevant support?*
> *If you are not, please do not worry. It is never too late to start the process.*
> *Are you inspiring your people, offering coaching and mentorship along the way?*
> *Have you established boundaries at work?*

Have you considered implementing healing strategies at work?
What could be some new metrics for you to assess the well-being of your people?

And most importantly, as a member of your own team, ask yourself:

Am I happy and experiencing a sense of flow at work?

Take time to self-check-in. Regularly. We are often caught up in our day-to-day and never-ending to-do list. Yet, taking time to reflect on the above questions, for example, will offer valuable insights as to where you are on your leadership journey. It will help you see what else can be done in the name of your *people*, and for yourself as a leader, so that you feel at your best, are at your best and produce your best work.

Part I

Key Takeaways

1 **Your Input Is Your Output**

- Start with *people* and prioritize their well-being; they are your organization's foundation.
- CX = EX: Your customer experience mirrors your employee experience.
- Focus on quality over quantity.

FlowBite: *Your people are your brand's engine.*

2 **Dare to Care**

- Well-being promotes performance: Commercial success hinges on investing in your *people*.
- Challenge the norm: Transition from a top-down to a nurturing leadership for organizational success.
- Caring time: Dare to care for your *people* (and yourself) as a leader. Leadership is not about being in charge. It is about taking care of those in your charge.

FlowBite: *Lead with care; inspire greatness.*

3 **Ask the Right Questions: Let Us Talk about Needs**

- Know your *people:* Ask meaningful questions. Get to know their needs and aspirations.
- Ignite *purpose*: Identify emotional triggers and what excites your *people*.

- Drive *performance*: Understanding and meeting your team's needs enhance performance.

FlowBite: *Understand your people; it begins with meeting their needs.*

4 **Equip Your People for Success**

- Reposition training: Promote training as a performance enabler, not an information dump.
- Embrace 'edutainment': Blend education with entertainment to create engaging and long-lasting learning experiences.

FlowBite: *Empower your teams with effective training and development strategies to fuel success and performance.*

5 **Coach to Empower**

- Coach for empowerment: Provide tools, skills and guidance for high-quality decision-making and cohesive teamwork.
- Stay on course: Resist the temptation to give in and trust in coaching's long-term positive impact.
- Seek mentorship for yourself: Embrace continuous learning and growth.

FlowBite: *Effective coaching empowers individuals, unites teams and drives success.*

6 **Establish Firm Boundaries: Create a Healthy Work Environment**

- Act as/be a flow leader: Inspire change and emphasize the importance of boundaries for achieving team harmony.
- Create a 'boundary manifesto': Mutual agreement on openly shared boundaries promotes clarity, understanding and respect within a team.

- Enhance team effectiveness: Enforcing the 'boundary manifesto' is crucial for teams to function effectively.

FlowBite: *Set firm boundaries for focus, team effectiveness and a healthy work environment.*

7 **Bring Healing Strategies to Your Workplace**

- Humanize the workplace: Address healing strategies openly to bring more empathy to the workplace.
- Embrace the uncomfortable: Bringing taboo topics to the surface uncovers latent needs that require attention. Sharing stories can initiate the healing process for both storytellers and listeners.
- Give healing its own spot: Acknowledge the necessity of time for recovery and healing from physical, mental or emotional pain. Employee performance thrives when they feel whole. Provide healing time to support recovery and well-being – a key leadership move for an emotionally intelligent business.

FlowBite: *Holistic healing strategies – your workplace enhancer and performance booster.*

8 **Reconsider Your Current Metrics and KPIs**

- Break the mould: Establish a healthier working culture by rethinking metrics and KPIs.
- Prioritize feedback: Use pulse surveys and open feedback platforms to gather insights beyond NPS scores.
- Analyse your employee experience (EX): Deep dive the various aspects of your EX to drive improvements.

FlowBite: *Shift to people-centric KPIs and feedback to boost success and performance.*

9 **Reflect on Your *Flow Leadership* Journey**

- Leadership is about inspiring and enabling others, focusing on input for meaningful output.
- Embody 'dare to care' leadership motto for your team and yourself.
- Discover your needs and the ones of your teams to provide the right support.
- Empower your *people* through coaching: Empower your team members.
- Set clear boundaries for yourself and your teams to maintain a healthy work environment.
- Implement healing strategies or mental wellness days to promote well-being at work.
- Introduce new metrics focused on assessing your employee well-being and feelings.
- Take time for self-check-in.
- Find your FLOW@WORK by reflecting on your emotional state at work.

FlowBite: *Leading with care begins by caring for oneself.*

Part II

Purpose

10

Bringing *Purpose* to the Workplace

More than ever before, people are seeking meaning at work. Employees are *more than ever* now willing to jump ship when they feel something is missing. They hop from *employer to employer* until they find a company that feels right for them. They do so until they discover a workplace and a position that enriches their body, mind and soul.

Quitting a job to protect one's well-being is *no longer taboo*; for younger generations, quitting to find purpose is now celebrated. What used to be *crazy, irresponsible and too risky* is now seen as bold, respected and inspiring. People come first. They choose themselves over anything else. This new reality provides the perfect opportunity to bring purposeful engagement within the workplace.

When leaders care enough for their people and themselves, they take a crucial step in beginning that transformation. They move from a top-down vertical type of leadership to a nurturing horizontal one. To make the shift happen, leaders must let go of their *armor* and *traditional belief system*. They must not be afraid to remove their helmets, show up as themselves and embrace their vulnerabilities. By showing their true colors, they will inspire others to do the same. Those leaders usually seek purpose for themselves and as a result bring purpose to their teams. As we have seen earlier on, it all starts with you as a leader.

To find meaning at work, people are willing to put in the work. And if people individually commit to becoming the best version of themselves, the expectation is that the company and its leaders will also have to do the work. Failing this introspection, the transformation can not happen. And without transforming the workplace, there will be an automatic and inevitable mismatch between the people and the companies.

Organizations will remain static and archaic, diminishing the attractiveness and retention of its people; meanwhile, the people will keep on evolving. Motion versus inertia is the dilemma that today's leaders are facing.

To achieve change, both the company and the individuals must commit to doing the work. Only together will they create a new environment, mindset and culture. The same process that an individual will follow to evolve, grow wiser and become more aware is applicable to organizations. An organization should build self-awareness and, as a first step, acknowledge what it is.

This is a key step in the 'healing' process. The transformation of an organization cannot happen unless there is simple acceptance and acknowledgement of what it is – what is the current state of things. The lightbulb moment is when as a leader you finally get it, when you see that first step towards change – that is what sets the system in motion.

Painting a clear and fair picture of the current reality enables the system to settle and move forward. At an individual level, we refer to this stage as releasing the trauma, the blockages, the fear and shadows. This verbalized acknowledgement positions the leaders and companies as trustworthy. A new chapter with a more 'heart-centric' communication can then start. This requires courage and humility.

A *healthy organization* is one that can cope with organizational change without affecting the motivation and morale of its people. A *sick organization* is, on the opposite, unable to cope, resulting in increased staff turnover, low motivation and morale. When this happens, the company wants to fix its *people* and provide individual coaching and personal development plans. However, *has the illness been diagnosed correctly?* Is that the answer? If the team is only one subgroup of the bigger system, the situation will remain. And without curing the root cause of the illness, the *sickness* will continue to spread.

This is the reason why tandem work between the *people* and the *system* is the answer.

No matter how an individual might perform and fully align to their values and life's mission, if the system is not healthy, positive changes will not take.

At an individual level, the best tools to do the work are our mind, body and soul. Most importantly, our bodies remember where we have been and are a rich source of information and insight. Staying anchored in our body, our physical self, is paramount to ensuring our connection to the overall system.

At an organization level, answers lie within the information its people hold and the system. Working at the individual level, although essential, will not suffice. The system needs to be looked upon each layer – the individual, team and organization. Failing to do so, crucial information and knowledge will be missed. Further, if we fix individuals but an issue remains within the dynamic of the system itself, then the problems will continue, perhaps with someone or something else.

The responsibility of leaders is to not only care and focus on the first 'P', *people,* but to bring *purpose* to the workplace. While your *people* are the foundation, your second 'P', *purpose*, provides a sense of direction. It serves as a North Star. It will guide your teams' actions and decisions (Figure 10.1).

Purpose is a powerful catalyst that will generate FLOW@WORK, because people are inherently drawn to meaningful work. A clear sense of *purpose* will provide your *people* with a deeper connection to their work and roles. This is how as a flow leader you can instill a feeling of fulfillment, provide meaning and generate intrinsic motivation. A *purpose-driven* team is more resilient, engaged and dedicated to the organization and its mission.

Figure 10.1 Fulfillment through FLOW@WORK: Reaching the North Star Together

When personal values align with professional aspirations, it fosters a fulfilling work environment. Individuals and teams in *flow* are driven by a shared sense of *purpose*, which naturally leads towards the third 'P', *performance.* This upward motion represents the collective energy and drive towards achieving exceptional outcomes.

And to get there, your role is crucial. You will need to take your team on a journey to finding *purpose.* Show the broader impact of your *people*'s work and how it ties into a larger vision that extends beyond their day-to-day tasks or projects. A shared *purpose* is what will unite your team members around a common goal. This is what will foster a sense of belonging and commitment. When people believe in a purpose, they become more passionate about their roles. This in turn leads to increased creativity, dedication, perseverance and productivity.

Finding purpose, for my teams and myself, has always been my biggest driver at work. Only later was I able to articulate that this quest was nothing less than finding FLOW@WORK. When your team is content within themselves, they will enter a zone of maximum performance and ultimate happiness. When they reach FLOW@WORK, a world of endless possibilities will open. Their outlook on their job and life expands, and potential obstacles are transcended. Energy flows, alignment kicks in, and value is generated.

Prior to going any further, may I encourage you to take a moment and reflect on the following?

Do you know your company's purpose? If so, what is it?
Do you know your team's purpose? If so, what is it?
Do you know what your purpose at work is? If so, what is it?

Are your people aware of your company's purpose?

Do they know what their purpose at work is?

If you have been able to answer most of these questions, you are off to a fantastic start. To ensure that your team is on the same page, it may be worthwhile asking them the same set of questions. Oftentimes, these questions trigger confusion. Over the years, I have witnessed the same story unfold so many times. When I enquire if people know their company or their team's purpose, everyone seems to know. The answer is most often the same: "Yes, of course we know!"

Smiles usually fade when the second question is asked: "Great! Then please tell me what it is, and what role you play in achieving that purpose." At this stage, team members usually start to look around, uncomfortable. Very few can clearly articulate it, if any. Questions are then asked, and a debate usually follows. Is she referring to our brand mission, a commercial mission, or our team mission? What does she mean?

What I learned throughout the process of clarifying *Purpose* is that teams usually know about the commercial ambitions of the company. Teams are, however, not versed as to what the company's purpose is. They are even less aware of how their roles contribute to the bigger purpose of the company. Which means that they have not been able yet to find their own purpose at work, as individuals.

Figure 10.2 Igniting Passion: Energizing Teams through Purpose-Driven Leadership

Leaders who can inspire their people with a compelling purpose will ignite passion and encourage FLOW@WORK to flourish. Purpose-driven work is a source of energy. It energises individuals and teams, leading to increased focus, perseverance, and FLOW@WORK (Figure 10.2).

11

What Does *Purpose* Mean for Your *People*?

As we have seen, people seek meaning and purpose at work. Of course, employees value salary, benefits and company leadership, but meaningful work drives job satisfaction more than ever. People spend one third of their lives working. Most of us spend eight hours a day, five days a week at work, equalling to about 40 hours a week. That is a large amount of time. People spend more time working than with their families, friends or doing things they love. So, if people spend so much time and energy at work, they may as well enjoy what they do. Would you not agree?

The ability to spend time doing a meaningful job is what truly energizes people. And the quest to find this meaningful work drives job satisfaction. Many managers would be surprised about how much this is valued, more so than what would be considered traditional perks.

Meaningful, engaging work not only fuels teams' professional achievements but also contributes to the growth of the organization and its people. As an employer, when people find meaning at work, and ultimately in life overall, the benefits pay off. People enter a feel-good zone. They find FLOW@WORK and, as a result, are more focused and exhibit increased job satisfaction, resulting in improved performance and productivity. More than that, they bring value at work and are less likely to quit (Figure 11.1).

Unfortunately, the reality is that many employees still feel like meaning is missing at work. Therefore, as the flow leaders that you are, the question should be:

How can I help my people find purpose at work?

Figure 11.1 Growing Together: Cultivating Meaningful Work for Thriving Teams

Meaningful work is work that makes an employee feel as if their job makes a difference and positively impacts society. The concept of meaningful work is universal. The ways in which employees find meaning in their jobs will vary and evolve over time. Your purpose today may be different than your purpose tomorrow or in a few years. Researching how your people define meaningful work at this moment in time is the first step.

To design an organization with purpose, the work needs to be done on the three layers of the *Flow Leadership* triangle. When people have found meaning at an individual level, the natural progression is towards teams and the overall collective of the organization.

Finding *Purpose* at the Individual Level – the First Layer of the *Flow Leadership* Triangle

Finding purpose at the individual level is to first identify what really matters to your people. What matters is often anchored in a personal belief system and value framework. When values and beliefs can be applied at work, purpose can be found. Imagine now if, on top of this, people were able to find ways to integrate their passions at work. How powerful could this be? A great starting point would be to know what those passions are. Unfortunately, many people are not aware of what brings them enjoyment. At work, the more they learn about their role, the company or industry, the more exposed they are to a new environment, the more it can pique their curiosity. When this happens, it ignites a spark for a newly found passion, source of energy and direction.

Most importantly, purpose comes from the outlook people have on their lives – their perspectives. Imagine two individuals who have the same job. One looks at *what* their job is, and the other looks at their job beyond the *what*, paying attention to the overall context, and how their job fits into this context.

For example, if their job is to clean toilets in a hospital, the first individual will see it as a pure cleaning job, a task to be completed. The other will see beyond the cleaning job and make meaning of what their job is. For that individual, ensuring a clean and welcoming environment is their way to help and ease the pain of those coming to such a place. It is a way to make sure that there is less risk of infection for a vulnerable patient. Beyond the *what*, the *how* matters for this individual (Figure 11.2).

Figure 11.2 Looking Deeper: Discovering Meaning Beyond the Task

Their job is no longer a job. It is a role, and, in this case, their role has meaning and purpose as it contributes towards helping others feel better. People have the power to find meaning and purpose in any job. It is all dependent on perspective.

In the example shared above, as for any others, finding purpose is about transcending the self and feeling connected to something bigger. It is about knowing the contribution and understanding the impact their work has on others.

So let us jump straight in. Grab a pen and notebook or open your laptop. Choose whatever is your preferred way to journal, reflect and take notes. When you are ready, we will start focusing on values and why they are important. Then, we will look at ways to identify passions and, lastly, discuss how to operate a shift in perspective to help make meaning of a current job reality.

Your Values

Values are fundamental principles that guide people's behaviour, choices and interactions with others. They shape people's identity and perception. Values are dynamic and can shift over time. When people are aware of their values, they can look for companies with similar values. This is a great way to find meaning at work. So let me ask you:

What are your values? Please list them out.

Feeling stuck? Here are some examples of values – learning, growth, accountability, loyalty, fairness, recognition, respect, honesty, transparency, authenticity, autonomy, teamwork, punctuality, positivity, a can-do mindset, reliability, the search for excellence, attention to details, achievement, work–life balance, making a difference, commitment and trust.

For each of those values you listed above, attribute a score between 1 and 10, with 10 being the most important.
Only keep the values with a score higher than 5.
Finally, rank these values by order of importance, and use them as guiding principles.

When people know their values, they can make the right career choices. Let us see how. Take a step back and ponder:

Are your values aligned with those of your company?

When your values seem at odds with your company's, this misalignment may generate a lack of motivation, a sense of feeling disconnected or frustration in your daily job. Recognizing this misalignment is the first step towards understanding the source of these feelings and generating the desire to initiate a positive change.

Staying in a job if there is a conflict between individual and company values can have both short- and long-term consequences. Some may choose to stay due to fear of change, but the impact on their well-being and identity can be profound. Staying when suffering may create emotional dissonance, reduce job satisfaction and, unfortunately, lead to intense stress or even burn-out. Over time, a person may even suffer from identity erosion as personal values are compromised for the sake of job security. The deterioration of mental health may lead to health challenges. The level of dissatisfaction and resentment towards the company may result in employees becoming completely unengaged.

In my own journey, I had the privilege of working in roles that felt more like a passionate pursuit than a traditional job. Each day brought a sense of joy and enthusiasm, with the company serving as a strong supporter, making challenges enjoyable. However, in one of those roles, as time progressed, I began to sense a shift – not in the company's support, but in my own aspirations versus the current path I was on. As time passed, I started to witness a gradual misalignment between my personal values and the company's proclaimed values.

While on paper, the company values had not changed, to me it felt as if their adherence to these stated values deviated over time. Trust and the perception of equal treatment, both fundamental values of mine, were shattered as career discussions went unfulfilled. Despite a prolonged effort to reconcile my personal values with this new reality, the misalignment became untenable. The decision to resign was not just a professional choice, it was an act to reclaim my own values and integrity.

Reflecting, I am grateful for the experience, where every day felt like a blend of passion and growth. Yet I reached a point where my goals and values were heading in a different direction. It is a bit like a relationship where you still care, but you realize you are moving in separate ways. Leaving was not just a job decision; it was about staying true to what mattered to me. It was a moment to make a choice and embrace change. These moments challenge us to think about what is important, question the way things are, and find a path that truly matches our values, goals and purpose. It is about discovering who we are and what really matters. It is a journey of self-discovery, resilience and the pursuit for authentic purpose.

This personal story underscores the importance of being attuned to the evolving alignment of personal and company values. It highlights the long-term consequences of neglecting such misalignments, not only for individual well-being but also for the overall health and trust within the organization.

In contrast, imagine a scenario where your values are aligned with those of the company. In this seamless alignment, your work feels purposeful and your contributions effortless. As both your and your company's values align, the process becomes a unified driving force for both your personal and company's success.

Do You Bring Your Passion to Work?

More than ever before, companies need passionate workers. Being passionate generates extreme drive, which leads to exponential performance and growth. This is much needed in today's rapidly changing business realities. The downside is that companies worry about investing in passionate workers because those workers are perceived as unstable due to their constant need for new challenges and learning opportunities.

Throughout my career, I was always one of those passionate employees who did not wait for opportunities to be handed to me. Instead, I took the initiative to seek out challenges and create new opportunities. I consistently looked for ways to contribute by generating fresh ideas, taking on new projects and volunteering for assignments that others might overlook. My proactive approach allowed me to grow and develop in ways that went beyond my regular job responsibilities, leading to both personal and professional growth.

For employees who might not know how to take such initiative, there is a simple and effective solution. As an employer, you can facilitate this by creating a 'bank of ideas' where ongoing projects and innovative concepts can be stored. This repository can include projects that never saw the light of day due to time constraints or shifting priorities. Passionate workers can then choose from these ideas and take ownership of them, bringing new energy and perspective to the table.

Additionally, consider offering a list of short-term assignments abroad or within different departments. These assignments provide employees with unique experiences and challenges, helping them grow while contributing to the company's global and cross-functional goals. Beyond the obvious benefits of career progression and succession planning, these initiatives can keep employees engaged and motivated by constantly providing them with exciting new challenges and learning opportunities. This approach not only fosters a culture of innovation and proactivity but also ensures that passionate employees are continuously inspired and valued.

Imagine what it would bring to an organization if people never felt like work was work. Imagine an employee waking up every morning feeling passionate and motivated to go to work. When at work, this employee is the one who will drive your business forward. Always on the lookout for opportunity to grow – that same employee will challenge the status quo and be creative and innovative when it comes to problem-solving, taking meaningful risks for enhanced performance.

Passionate workers are more than happy. They are animated by this intrinsic need to do better and, as a result, boost performance. Their thirst for new ideas often brings them beyond their core responsibilities. In doing so, they push boundaries, learn new skills and move the organization forward. To them, growth comes in many ways and often through their network. They connect with others to learn from experts and build new knowledge to perform better.

Your role as a flow leader is to ignite those passions. In our next chapter, 'What is FLOW@WORK', you will learn the process to help your people identify their passions and how you can facilitate for your people meaningful work that taps into those passions. Having the right people in the right place and at the right level of challenge is essential, as it will bring people into a zone of natural excellence.

Interested to better understand what your passions are? Why don't you take a few minutes and ask yourself the following questions?

> *How do you want to spend your life at work?*
> *What brings you joy and lights you up from within?*
> *What are the activities that you love doing when at work?*
> *If you are unsure, what are the activities that you love doing when not at work? List them out.*
> *What is your dream job?*
> *What does it look like?*
> *What activities would it require you to pursue?*
> *If you could start all over again, what work would you do now?*

Take the time to read all your answers. From those answers, identify what your passions are. Write them down on individual pieces of paper. Display them in front of you. Take the first one in your hand, close your eyes and ask yourself:

> *How does this passion (name it) make me feel?*
> *What is so important for me about this passion?*
> *Give it a score ranging from 1 to 10 – 10 being of most importance.*
> *Repeat the exercise until all your papers are organized by order of importance.*

Those are your passions – what drives you from inside. The challenge is to then know how to bring some of them to work.

Since I was a little girl, all I wanted was to heal the world and the people. I wanted to take away pain and create a world where everyone is happy. In a corporate world, that burning desire translated into being of service to my company, my people and my clients. More specifically, I understood that the reason why I loved leading is that I could take care of my people. In the process, I also understood that in designing the best customer experience, I could care for my clients. And that in searching for new ways of doing, I could serve my company better. Through this day to day, I was able to make a difference in people's lives. And for me, that was my reason to be. My passion. My source of growth and inspiration.

Now that you have read the above, ask yourself again the same question:

What are my passions?
And how can I bring them to work?

You are the main character of your own destiny. You have the power to shape it in any way or form you wish. Do not wait. Go and create what could become yours.

Shifting Your Perspective

People have the power to reframe their perspective at any point. When you change the way you look at things, it is easier to find meaning and purpose. The challenge is to come from a place of ownership of one's reality.

Over the past 20 years of coaching and workshop delivery, too often I heard people say, 'Things will never change.' They blame the status quo on others, on the company, on external factors that they claim to have no control over. The reality is nothing further from the truth.

When things go south, people have a choice. To stay, usually feeling stuck, or to take a risk and change their situation. Change requires courage, and often people prefer to remain stuck because this is the easy road. It is less scary to complain about what is wrong, play the blame game, than to own the change and take risks. However, by shifting perspective and claiming ownership, and ultimately our own power, people can liberate themselves and find purpose.

Take a moment and answer the questions below . . . honestly. Your heart knows the truth, so let it be your guide for this exercise.

Do you feel stuck at work?
Do you feel tired and demotivated?
Do you dread going to work?
Do you feel like you have no control over what is happening to you?
Do you blame others for what is happening in the organization and your unhappiness at work?
Do you spend a considerable amount of time talking about what is not working?
Do you wish you were doing something else?

If you have answered 'yes' to most of those questions, let me reiterate – it does not have to be that way. Let us work on how shifting your perspective can bring real change to your reality.

To start, close your eyes and try to visualize a new reality at work that would flip the answers to your questions above. Imagine doing this, one step at the time. Can you see it?

What does your new reality at work look like?
What comes to mind?

Then hold on to that new vision and try to feel it:

How does it make your feel?
What are the feelings coming through?
What type of energy does it bring?

Can you see the vision in more details? Try to picture it:

Where are you?
In that same organization or somewhere else? If so, where?
How is this new environment of yours?
Do you hear sound?
Do you see colours?

And lastly, can you contextualize it?

What job are you doing?

By completing this exercise, you may find the strength to embark on your own journey. Finding purpose is not straightforward. It requires patience and diligence. And once you find it, it will be the most rewarding accomplishment. Manifest your vision. Give it a try. You can do it.

Finding *Purpose* at the Team Level – the Second Layer of the *Flow Leadership* Triangle

As a leader, your job is to help your people find their purpose at an individual and team level. One way to start is to try to define with your people a clear team mission statement that aligns with your company's purpose. 79% of business leaders believe that purpose is essential for success in business. According to a PWC study titled *Putting Purpose to Work*, only 34% of leadership decisions are guided by organizational purpose.

If you are ready to do this exercise, follow the steps hereafter. The first part is focused on the team and functions, and the second part is focused on the individual.

Step One – Team Focus

The first step to finding purpose at the team level is to reflect on your company's purpose. Then, try to establish what your company's mission and values are to understand how your teams' goal contributes to the broader purpose.

Go further by conducting a group brainwriting session to identify the specific impact your team aims to achieve and the value it brings to the organization. Once this is completed, you will be able to start crafting a team mission statement.

Based on the brainwriting, collaboratively create a clear and concise team mission statement that encapsulates the team's purpose and objectives. When all agree, share it and schedule a follow-up meeting.

Once *everyone* is comfortable with the mission statement, share the final version with all team members and regularly revisit it during team meetings to ensure continued alignment.

Step Two – Individual Focus

Inspire your people to create their own purpose slogan for their role and contributions. This goes beyond the nature of the job title, which is static and often quite dry. Let your people be creative. Make them see how their individual purpose is contributing towards the purpose of the organization.

Once this is done, ask each of your team members to share their purpose slogan in front of their peers. Collect each purpose slogan. Create a purpose *collage* with three circles. At the centre, place your company's purpose. In the next circle, place your teams' purpose.

And in the outer circle, place the individual purpose slogan of each of your team members.

Those are a few thoughts on how to bring purpose to your people and teams. In the next chapter, we will explore what else can be done.

12

What is FLOW@WORK?

Flow is a word that is simple yet so powerful. In just four letters emerges a concept that could drastically enhance the workplace. Just writing this word down actually gives me goosebumps.

What is *flow*, you may wonder?

Sometimes referred to as *being in the zone, being on the ball* or having *found your groove, flow* is a state of mind that brings together cognitive, physiological and affective aspects. It could simply refer to the optimal psychophysical state. In a nutshell, it is a mental state. Wikipedia: 'Flow is characterized by the complete absorption in what one does, and a resulting transformation in one's sense of time.'

The *flow* state theory was developed by Mihály Csíkszentmihályi in 1975 based on research he did when examining people who did activities for pleasure, even when they were not rewarded with money or fame. He researched artists, discovering that enjoyment did not result from relaxing or living without stress, but during these intense activities in which their attention was fully absorbed. He called this state *flow* because, during his research, people illustrated their intense experiences using the metaphor of being carried by a current like the flow of a river. *Flow* can lead to experiencing life more fully and intensely. It brings more meaning and can strengthen how we define who we are.

Unfortunately, many people with careers in the corporate world feel a deep longing and disconnection between who they truly are and their corporate persona. Over the years and to fit in, leaders have developed different personas. Yet, to find meaning and bring purpose to the workplace, the process starts with reconnecting to the true essence of who we are. It is about shedding the layers and reintegrating your personas. It is about showing your true colours

(Figure 12.1). And my goal is to help you bridge the gap, embrace your spirit and begin to have a more humane experience within this heavily structured environment.

Figure 12.1 Reconnect to Your Essence: Paint Your True Colours in the Corporate World

Today's leaders have a crucial role in creating an environment that nurtures *flow*, enabling employees to experience the joy of being fully engaged in their work. By prioritizing the well-being of their *people*, fostering a sense of *purpose* and promoting continuous growth and performance excellence, companies can cultivate a flow-promoting culture that not only enhances productivity but also raises employee satisfaction and overall well-being.

Embracing the power of the 3Ps – *People, Purpose* and *Performance* – can lead to a workplace where *flow* becomes a natural and transformative state, unlocking the full potential of individuals, teams and their system.

Imagine a workplace where your team members are fully immersed in their work. Picture a team experiencing a state of complete focus. Visualize that same team energized by their work and together achieving unrivalled performances effortlessly. This is FLOW@WORK – the holy trinity of productivity, team efficiencies and engagement in the workplace.

Although corporate culture is sometimes stuffy and restrictive, my goal is to infuse it with greater humanity, purpose and contentment. Why should your teams not love what they do? My mission is to show you how this is possible and to give leaders and teams new ways to achieve FLOW@WORK.

Leaders will benefit from these field-tested insights into how personal development and self-work are the first steps to becoming a flow leader, with the mental immunity to handle team challenges with empathy and compassion. As leaders, you may have been taught to assess your people through their performance. The wisest thing to do is to move away from KPIs and look at the holistic output of the person – their mental health, their emotional balance, their *flow* level. Because this approach generates exponential positive returns.

When you are in *flow*, you have endless energy, and you do what you love in a way that makes you the best at what you do. This can be especially important for a leader to work towards.

Beyond *flow*, an employee can experience different emotions at work. Arousal, for example, is a state that someone often feels outside of their comfort zone. Yet arousal can easily turn into anxiety, inducing a sense of being overwhelmed and, eventually, burn-out. This is often what a newcomer will experience or when an employee takes on a new role and challenge. This can lead one to be in a constant state of anxiety, which brings out the opposite of productivity, empathy and creativity.

On the other end of the spectrum of emotions, imagine someone who has been in the same role and function for a very long time. Boredom and loss of *flow* could occur if that person is unable to find meaning in their role and, over time, becomes dissatisfied.

Regardless of your employees' states of being, as a leader you can start moving your people towards FLOW@WORK. Remember, nothing is set in stone. Everything is in motion. Your role as a flow leader is to identify what needs to be done, to put the plan into action and to bring your people into their *flow* (Figure 12.2).

Figure 12.2 Charting the Course: Guiding Your Team Towards New Horizons of Flow

Steven Kotler, *The New York Times* bestselling author, award-winning journalist and executive director of the Flow Research Collective, explains the neurochemical changes that occur during the *flow* state. He describes this optimal state of consciousness as strengthening motivation, creativity and learning. Kotler is one of my heroes and mentors, without his knowing it! He has given me hope that *flow* is a topic that companies and individuals alike should embrace and believe in. You can listen to his *Flow Research Collective Radio*, a top ten iTunes science podcast.

In the multimedia web portal Big Think's YouTube video, 'The Neurochemistry of Flow States for Big Think', Steven Kotler explains, 'The brain produces a giant cascade of neurochemistry. You get norepinephrine, dopamine, anandamide, serotonin, and endorphins. All five of these are performance enhancing neurochemicals.' In fact, this explosive mix helps us keep our focus, and *flow* occurs in the zone between stress and performance.

The employee that manages to hit that zone strikes the perfect score and perfect balance between the level of challenges and skills. There is a feeling of timelessness, which leads to natural excellence. The task seems easy, and things just *come together*. Experiencing FLOW@WORK induces your team to fully engage in the activity and remain focused with heightened absorption and concentration. 'The happiest people are so involved in an activity that nothing else seems to matter; the experience itself is so enjoyable that people will do it even at a great cost,' so writes Mihaly Csikszentmihalyi, Hungarian–American psychologist and concept creator of the flow theory.

When employees are not engaged at work, it feels as if their jobs are simply something they must do. They often feel that they are investing time and energy in achieving someone else's goals. Instead, when clear goals are explained, employees feel empowered to do their best and find purpose.

When employees know how they are doing, it is easier for them to maintain focus and readjust. Feedback is not only about performance. Feedback should be focused on recognition, mentoring and coaching to further fuel the employees' engagement. Feedback should be in the moment or else ego gets in the way. This is why performance reviews should be ongoing and regular.

Balancing the right level of challenge and skill is key and can be easily measured. When the employees' skills match their challenges, they will perform at their best. When their skills exceed their challenges, they will be bored. And when the challenge is too high, they will be stressed. As human beings, when we are stressed, the body releases large amounts of cortisol. When employees are aware of their strengths, the leaders and the employees can see how to best match the capabilities required to do their job within the team framework.

When employees are in the state of FLOW@WORK, their consciousness becomes one with what they are doing. Such a state can be achieved only if the task is challenging enough to require the mobilization of personal skills, promoting concentration and engagement. When employees are in the zone, their involvement in a challenging task and being in the present is like a laser focus. Distractions are not seen or heard. This state allows for information to be retained and integrated.

For the team FLOW@WORK to occur, it is all about setting the right foundation. It is about ensuring that each employee individually and collectively find their FLOW@WORK. When the team has found it, it is then ready to respond to external and internal pressure and challenges in the best way, resulting in the best team output. In fact, the most effective business teams know how to balance tensions. They create synergies between members, developing individual and team efficiencies. Performing at their best, when challenges (which are inevitable) appear, the team's response will make all the difference because, in the process, they have built on the first foundation for a team to perform: Trust.

Team FLOW@WORK occurs when team members listen closely to each other, work in unison towards one objective and communicate openly so that everyone gets immediate feedback.

For the team FLOW@WORK to emerge, there must be a collective ambition, a clear mission along with aligned personal goals, the right match of skills to the challenge, an open communication, a safe space, and mutual commitment and dedication. This is what will create the spark, foster trust and FLOW@WORK in your workplace.

Bringing FLOW@WORK to the workplace will generate many benefits. Individuals are provided with the opportunity to do what they do best, and companies reap the benefits, to name a few: higher productivity, lower turnover, greater profit, customer satisfaction and workplace safety. For the teams, it will provide increased team efficiency, a sense of being in it together (unity), co-accountability, trust and focus. The level of concentration, motivation, engagement, involvement or the degree to which individuals are positively stretched contributes to the experience of well-being at work, leading them to be *in the zone*.

While the state of FLOW@WORK increases productivity, information processing and problem-solving, individuals who are in the zone of FLOW@WORK will have higher engagement and higher retention and will create greater customer satisfaction.

Most importantly, FLOW@WORK will contribute to a healthy workplace culture. It is about creating the right culture for the right mindset! Over the years, I cannot

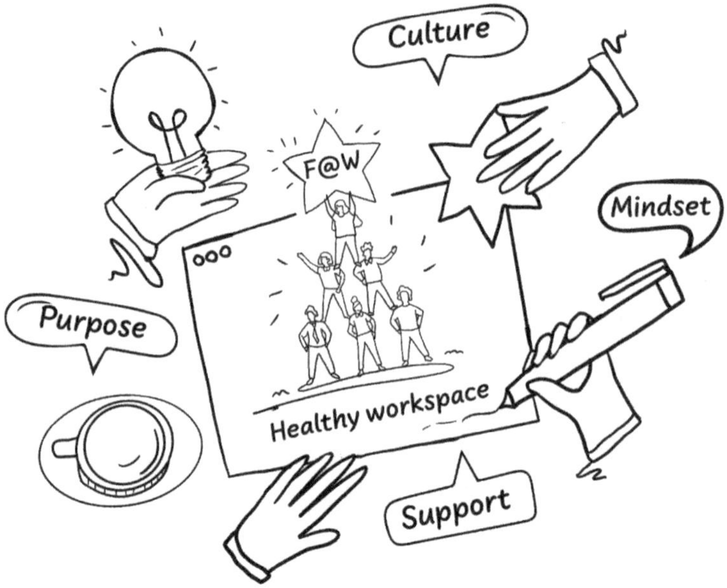

Figure 12.3 Constructing a Healthy Workplace: The Pyramid of Thriving Teams

recall how many times I have heard, 'We need a mindset change.' The reality is that you cannot just click your fingers and change your mindset. What needs to be done goes far beyond any team social gathering. As leaders, you need to create the right nurturing and growth culture for your teams so that every individual can thrive. Your role is essential. You are the head coach for your team. And you can bring them into FLOW@WORK (Figure 12.3).

13

Design Your FLOW@WORK Workshop Series

If you are ready to embark on this magical journey, as flow leaders you will need to focus on the first layer of the *flow leadership* triangle – the individuals and the second layer, your teams. This will ensure that you connect your first 2Ps – *people with purpose.*

At the individual level, the key is to not only care for your people, as we have seen in Part I. It is about caring in a relevant way – in understanding what drives them. Throughout this process, your role is to identify what meaningful work looks like for each one of them. If you identify their professional ambitions and dreams, you have understood their intrinsic motivations. And when you do understand what motivates them, you can help them derive meaning from it and reach their objectives. The role of any leader is not only about delivering performance, it is also about bringing people into that place of knowing (Figure 13.1).

Figure 13.1 Gears of Purpose: Tools to Ignite the Engine of Meaning

To facilitate that knowing, one of the tools that I use the most, as part of a workshop series I designed, is called the 'blazon exercise'. For authenticity, trust and growth to exist, team members need to feel comfortable to be transparent and vulnerable with one another and with their leadership. One of the processes to get there is for each team member to be able to openly display their needs, motivations, weaknesses and strengths. In doing so, a powerful message is sent, shared and assimilated: 'we are all works in progress'. It illustrates that our life at work is a journey – a quest of some sorts to find meaning and purpose.

A team is a collective body, and the key is for individuals to be aware of how everyone can contribute differently to reach the team mission and find purpose. The end game is to cultivate such an environment as it triggers change and empowers individuals to seek *flow* and happiness. It helps people understand that they are the main characters of their own life at work. And while the system may not change, they can claim back their happiness at work. It is a matter of perspective.

Another tool that I use is an assessment of their flow level at work. It helps understand the emotions felt at work. There are nine states a person can be in, ranging from flow, control, boredom, detachment, apathy, arousal, anxiety, worry and indifference. More than that, it will show their reality versus what that person feels their reality is. And often, as you can guess, there is a disconnect. Therefore, the first step will be to bring that person into awareness *prior to* starting any work. In addition, this assessment helps better understand what the natural talents of each individual are and if those talents are used at the right frequency.

Tools like the 'blazon exercise' or the understanding of the team's *flow* level are powerful and should be handled with care (Figure 13.2). It cannot be implemented randomly. Rather, it should be part of a workshop process that aims to bring your people and teams into FLOW@WORK. Each part of the journey should be followed through with a proper action plan. This is critical for the outcome to unfold. Failing to do so, nothing will change. Remember, as a leader, you and your people will need to put in the work.

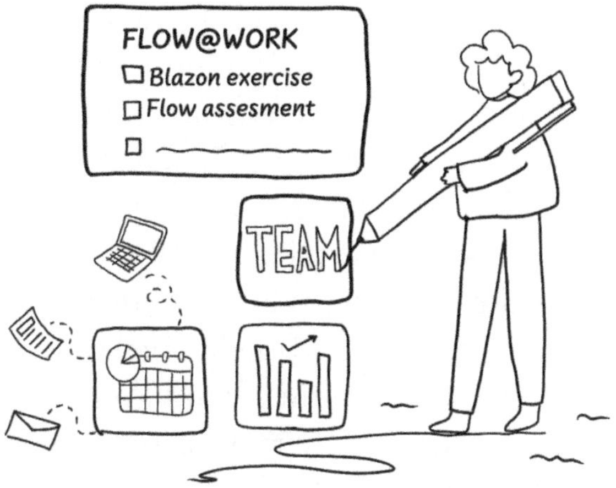

Figure 13.2 Scripting Success: Use Tools for Guiding Teams into Flow

According to a McKinsey study, 63% of employees expect their employers to provide opportunities to fulfil their purpose in their day-to-day work. As the flow leader that you are, look for ways to help your people live their purpose at work. Work on short-term and long-term actionable yearly plans. I am not a fan of only concentrating on a 5-year plan, as this is too far out in the reality of our lives today. Show your people the journey ahead and how to get there. In doing so, you help build purpose and motivation.

The moment you implement such tools as a leader, be warned that it will trigger introspective work on all fronts. It will bring to the surface your people's happiness or lack thereof at work. Some of your team members may come forward. Some may realize that they are not in *flow* in their current position. Through self-discovery, you may lose people.

The process can become an eye-opening moment when they realize that what they are doing is not what inspires them. And that is okay. It is part of the process. Whatever the reason is – whether a role changed and the possessed strengths and talents no longer match a role, or dissatisfaction with the work environment – be aware that it will cause a shift in perspective. When this happens, it is because the spark was created, and suddenly, your people and teams are eager to find their FLOW@WORK.

Thanks to the process, they will identify what they are after and then understand their talents, strengths and intrinsic motivations. When they hand their resignation to you, congratulate them on their decision and the courage they had to act upon their discovery. In chasing FLOW@WORK, they are going after their dreams, and this can only command your respect and support as flow leaders.

When you begin opening to your team, walls and barriers can quickly begin to crumble. You might find your team sharing things about their lives and journeys, what they are going through or what they are trying to achieve. A more honest environment begins to take shape with greater transparency. Some people will realize that they simply want to make a change and that is okay because it is good for them and it is good for you. You do not want someone who is not the right fit for your team. Other people may realize that they are not ready to be in this sphere of self-examination.

After this, however, is the moment the team begins to come together. The team begins to carry one another. It is this type of energy that is extremely transformative. This new team dynamic will motivate people to be better and grow.

Another reason why I included this cautionary note is that it can make you question your own process or your leadership skills. I personally experienced people leaving and could have stopped there and said, 'Maybe it is not a good workshop' or 'Maybe I am not the flow leader I aspire to be.' I did not because after having done many workshops, I have noticed the positive impact it had on so many over time.

The tools and this workshop process will give people clarity. They will question what their FLOW@WORK is and become in charge of their own happiness. Some may discover this process does not work for them, but this does not negate its intrinsic value and the positive impact it can have on many others.

The process can trigger reactions that are less than favourable for some people. For whatever reason (not wanting to work on self, a default of blaming others, a habit of rationalizing or an unflinching belief in a self-story), it can cause a negative reaction. Knowing this may occur can save you from significant doubt and stress as the process unfolds.

While some may leave, others will commit and stay. The ones that do will want to proceed with inner and outer work. When this happens, leave your door open for any team member to come forward. Coach them to find their FLOW@WORK. On many occasions, I had team members reaching out to me. And together, we embarked on a very rewarding mutual journey.

I will always remember the day an intern thanked me after one of our regular discussions and shared that he felt that his dopamine level (known as the happy hormone) had increased. Hearing such feedback brought tears to my eyes. I had managed to inspire an intern; there, standing in front of me, was the next generation of flow leaders.

When you spend time coaching your people, they will become faster, more competent and trusted right-hand helpers. They will be eager to grow and start asking relevant questions that will enable them to deliver more accurately and efficiently. In doing so, they will show others that asking the right questions gets things moving in the right direction. For those people, their ego is not in the way. As a result, others will start to dare to challenge themselves further.

As a leader, you should dare to care, and your teams should care to dare. To help them get there, one of the tools that I have designed is called 'pitch days'. They foster creativity and innovation. Anyone who has ideas that could serve our team and our purpose is encouraged to present. During one of the first editions, the only person who presented was an intern. She stood up, owned the stage and brilliantly shared her idea. What a hero! She inspired so many that day in caring to dare. The fact that an intern dared to do this signalled to the others that it was safe to take part in such an exercise. Soon after, many others followed.

Teams that work well together are teams that know each other. A shadowing programme can help break silos, increase empathy and create synergies between departments.

This will enable team members from different departments to explore what others do, how they do it and how their own work impacts others. A programme such as this could break cross-functional team barriers to enable an open dialogue and more productive conversations when objectives and agendas are different.

Think of what your company needs and what you as a flow leader suffer from the most within the dynamics of your teams. For example, in the retail/luxury industry, in order to provide the best customer experience, the boutique teams and customer service teams must usually work together to deliver this desired outcome. The reality in most cases is that these teams end up working in silos – without a coordinated effort, oftentimes the wrong message or experience is delivered to the customer. One way to build stronger relationships between teams is to have a shadowing or exchange programme. Having first-hand experience of each other's worlds and challenges will allow colleagues to find better ways to work with each other.

Now that you have started to focus on your first layer of the *flow leadership* triangle, it is time to move up to the team's layer. Teams are often composed of different subgroups, and the objective of a flow leader should be to bring them together to produce the best work in the best possible manner. In unison.

To start with, ask yourself the following questions:

Are my teams looking in the same direction?
Are my teams working together?
Are my teams feeling at their best?
Are my teams at their best?
Are my teams producing their best work?

Go one step further: reflect on how you have handled team mergers or the integration of different subgroups in the past to work on a common project. Ask yourself:

Did it work?
If it worked, what could I have done better?
If it did not work, what would I do differently?
Are there silos within the subgroups?

If you have had to handle this type of situation in the past, reflect on how you approached it. If you do not have any experience in this area, it is fine. Instead, ask yourself as a leader how you would proceed should you be given the challenge. There are many different options on how to operate the merger or integration of teams, subgroups or individuals. The following are only two approaches among many others. This is used to illustrate what *flow leadership* could look like in that very specific context.

One approach to handling teams' integration or mergers is more traditional. Think of it as a bit more autocratic and a solitary route. This is when the leader looks at organizational charts, plugs people where needed and establishes the team structure. It would then be shared with the team members. The leader in that instance retains sole ownership of the team structure. The advantages of such a method include a faster process, more efficiency due to the speed of reaction, a standardized and known approach, one sole decision-maker, less time spent in discussion and the possibility to proceed with business in a timely manner.

On the other hand, the disadvantage will arise from the difficulty to get the buy-in of the team member post decision, a lack of understanding of the team dynamics, failure to know the strengths, weaknesses and talents of everyone, risk of placing the wrong person in the wrong position, lack of awareness of individual needs, values and ways of working and imposter syndrome.

The opposite approach is through *flow leadership*. It is when you, as the leader, would make time for your people to understand who they are as both employees and human beings and invest in their talents and areas of development. It is a more inclusive way of handling a team merger or integration by reflecting a strong team spirit mindset.

Doing so will enable you to break silos, generate passion, excitement, energy and *flow*. This is the avenue to build your team knowledge and trust, create a safe place and understand the needs of the individual and the collective. Most importantly, it will enable you to engage in dialogue and create a feedback loop to discover the drivers of each team member and the overall team. It contributes to establishing your *flow leadership* style, gives everyone a voice and reveals unresolved team dynamics and latent issues.

Of course, there are challenges with this approach. Leading this way takes more of your time and energy. You will need trust and internal buy-in. Going down this road requires faith from your team members as there will be chaos before clarity, and for some, this methodology will not work, and you may lose some members along the way. And that is OK. It is sometimes par for the course. This road may be slower and more demanding, but the reward is significant. Consider it a smart investment.

Your first step in designing a FLOW@WORK workshop series is to be clear on your objectives – what it is that you are seeking and hoping to achieve. Each workshop *should be* gradual and build upon each other, progressively adding new elements. It should follow a pragmatic chronology of events, all designed to bring your teams, individually and collectively, into their FLOW@WORK. Think of this workshop series as a journey in time, starting before the first day of the workshop and continuing after.

Think of your first workshop as an icebreaker, a way to get acquainted. It should be about getting to know one another. There is a need to understand who your team is and who they are as individuals, more than understanding them as employees. Discovering their intrinsic motivations and assessing their level of happiness and *flow* are essential. Build this foundation first to better understand their strengths and energy.

Choose your space wisely. The environment needs to foster engagement. When hosting workshops in person, the preference is to find a big, open space – bright, airy, welcoming, with lots of windows. Even the layout of the chairs can send different messages. Set the scene. Look at it as a scenography or picture to paint. You are the maestro. The layout will positively influence the team dynamics and facilitate dialogues and exchanges. Drinks, food and room setup should be thought of. The room should be somehow 'dressed up'.

Over the years, what I learned is to never underestimate that the environment you create is the experience you convey. Look at every aspect, every detail. Think of it as the production of a show or event. As you would set the stage for customer experiences in a retail space, here you should do the same for your employees. Prepare both the workshop content and the setting well ahead of time. Rehearse, follow your agenda and keep track of time. Alternate sit-down and activity moments. Use the space. The atmosphere created will influence the outcome of your workshop.

Prior to your big day, check in and ponder the following.

Why am I doing this?
Am I clear on the objective of the workshop?
What emotions and feelings do I want to induce?
How do I respect the boundaries of individuals yet make them gel as a team?
How do I strike the right balance between people and business needs?
What can I do to maintain the level of energy and involvement throughout the day?
How do I make it a fun day to remember?
How will I know if I have achieved the desired outcome?

On the big day, you should feel prepared, eager to start and excited. Become an observer. Pay attention to what is not being said, but what you perceive. Proceed with deep listening beyond the words. Read body language. Decipher the emotions. Pay attention to the team dynamics. What is happening and what is NOT happening. Watch it as a scene unfolding. Absorb it all. Crucial information resides in nonverbal communication.

Watch and pay attention to how your teams behave, how they enter the room and how they pick their spots. It may be a revelation. Observing everyone, individually and collectively, will give you indications as to the level of team synergy or lack thereof. Most times, people will enter and act as separate teams.

After the first series of exercises (here you can use the 'blazon' and the *flow* assessment), usually the verdict becomes crystal clear and your assumptions should be validated. There will most likely be different subgroups. Very strong in their own ways, yet with siloes in between. Why? Simple. Each subgroup has their own vision, mission and perspective. It is as if they speak different languages and do not have a common one they can communicate through. The first workshop usually reveals this clumsy reality, which can be quite frustrating at times, but mostly, it is energy-draining and time-inefficient.

I am sure that this will resonate with some leaders out there. In the end, it all comes down to energy. Sometimes it exists and sometimes it does not. Creating the spark is the first step towards team efficiency and bringing FLOW@WORK. This is paramount to ensure that every participant feels co-responsible and co-accountable. The success of your workshop depends on it. The notion of blended learning, mixing elements of virtual and in-person meetings, creates the right balance and contributes to breaking the monotony.

For your next workshop, change the scenery and consider hosting this workshop outside of the office to provide a different vibe. This second stage is my favourite. It is the moment of truth. By this point, FLOW@WORK should have started to impact your teams. You may hear them laugh and see them exchanging. The energy level should be much higher than during your first workshop and you will feel as if the team you are looking at has transformed.

To your delight, when your teams sit down, they will most likely mix up. At that point, close your eyes, open them again and take in this beautiful sight. Here they are, sitting as one team, right in front of you. *Flow* by then will have become your buzzword and objective as a team. How could this happen? By inspiring them to be the change, share openly, maintain a transparent communication, express vulnerabilities and work towards finding their FLOW@WORK.

Even though by then your team's ecosystem will have drastically improved, there may still be some synergies missing for the full team to come together. This second workshop is designed for all team members to come together and remove the last barriers. Again, this could mean some more people may be triggered. And remember, that is okay and part of the process. To build the winning team, you need people to be fully in and committed to walk this path.

Utilize this second workshop to establish clear objectives, agree on your values, purpose and revised team structure. Design your team rules, establish an intra-team collaboration agreement to further foster team dynamics and remove any silos or barriers left.

Your last workshop, usually the third one (although sometimes more will be needed) will be the most rewarding of them all. Congratulations! By now you have reached the end of the series of workshops, and that should be cause for celebration. There is no better way than to host an offsite event to conclude your workshop series.

Gather your team, review the journey with them and reward them for a job well done. The objectives of this final get-together will be about reviewing your team values, team rules and contract of collaboration within teams, and seeking their feedback on who you are as a leader and the process undertaken thus far.

For you, as flow leader, it will be your reality check. It requires a lot of courage to stand in front of your team, asking them for honest feedback on areas that they consider your strengths and areas for improvement, and for you, in turn, to show your vulnerabilities. In doing so, as a flow leader you will illustrate that vulnerabilities are a source of growth, regardless of your seniority level. It will show others how willing you are to act on what you teach, and a bond will be created.

After this mission is complete, try to create the unexpected – expand on the notion of edutainment and experiential training. Immerse your teams in the power of the experience. If your team is front-facing with clients, an etiquette workshop disguised as a black-tie event is a creative way to treat your team as well as have them learning in motion. This type of event is the perfect opportunity to get to know each other even more. Learning in motion is a new concept, and, like learning through emotions, it is worth the investment.

The impact of such a workshop series will be greater if a follow-up phase is implemented. Consider rolling out a six-month group coaching programme dedicated to finding FLOW@WORK. Group coaching has a goal to support the implementation phase and ensure everyone is on track. It can be complemented with individual coaching sessions for those in need.

The workshop suggestions mentioned earlier can vary greatly depending on the objectives, circumstances and expectations. The process will be guided by the clarity on what you, as a leader, are trying to achieve with your team. The more you are aware of your needs, the better equipped you are to tackle the journey.

Throughout your workshop process, give your employees the opportunity to share their own stories. Finding FLOW@WORK can be turned into an internal podcast series for your people. Go beyond the norm. Release it externally and promote your working culture and stories. This is employee experience (EX) all the way. Explore the topics around *flow*, tips to find *flow*, well-being, work–life balance, teamwork, performance and happiness in the workplace. When launched, in most cases, the episodes will garner immediate interest. Keep the momentum going by releasing new episodes often and interviewing your employees on their journeys and personal stories.

Be creative. Follow where *flow* leads you and your teams.

14

It All Starts with You as Leaders

Prior to embarking on such a journey with your teams, take a moment to check in and better assess your leadership style:

Are you aware of how you lead?
Are you leading with your gut?
Are you listening to the brain in your heart?
Do you listen to its truth?
Do you pay attention to what feels right in your bones?
When was the last time you led with instinct?
Do you know your vulnerabilities?
Have you openly shared your vulnerabilities?
Are you clear on your boundaries and your needs?
Have you openly shared your boundaries and needs?
Have you found purpose and happiness at work?
Would you like to bring your teams in FLOW@WORK?

If you answer 'yes' or have answers to most of those questions, finding FLOW@WORK with your teams will be like second nature. If you answer 'no' to most of those questions, but you wished it was 'yes', finding FLOW@WORK will enable you to grow those *flow leadership* qualities. If you answer 'no' to most of them, and are satisfied with the answer, FLOW@WORK may not be the right journey for you to embark on just now. And that is okay! This concept is not for everyone.

All I know is that it is easy for teams to fall into autopilot, repeating the same conflicts and obstacles. And leaders sometimes need a co-navigator to help them introduce new paradigms, see team dynamics in a new light and build positive momentum to begin seeing life's opportunities rather than just obstacles. Begin to view team challenges from a place of strength and understanding. Life stressors and unresolved mindset issues can sabotage team cohesion and create gaps between leadership and staff. These are all common corporate obstacles that keep businesses from achieving greater successes. It is however possible to tap into your team's full potential by incorporating the principles of *flow*, energize your team and create flow leaders.

The question is, *are you ready to embark on the journey to finding FLOW@WORK?*

Bringing FLOW@WORK takes a unique approach to corporate coaching, working with both individuals and the group in the context of the team. With a focus on mindset and authentic growth, each session is a unique opportunity to create a renewed environment that fosters team unification and increased dedication and productivity. It will energize your team, bring purpose to the workplace and create an open environment that encourages creativity and communication. Wherever it has been implemented, the FLOW@WORK workshop series and the different *flow* and *3Ps* assessments have been a hit. Across the board, in different geographic locations, industries and settings, team efficiencies increased drastically, often from somewhere in the 20% range to the 70% mark in under a year – a phenomenal outcome.

In addition, witnessing the impact it had on the bottom line was reassuring and highly motivating for those who participated in this mission. By focusing on the first 2Ps (*people and purpose*), the business impact on *performance* was exponential. Focusing on your *people* and their *purpose* will give them the energy, belief and confidence to move forward and reach for the stars. Over the course of the workshops and all my coaching on individuals and teams around the world, what I realized throughout the years is that FLOW@WORK can enable *people* to find their FLOW4YOU (upcoming book!).

Regardless of the entry door, the work related to finding this *flow* state is what brings it to all areas of life. It brings in extraordinary results. This is how you hit your targets month after month, making the impossible possible when you need to reach your target, for example. I vividly recall the exhilarating times when my teams and I were trying to close budgets throughout our network of boutiques in North America. As a team, rowing in the same direction, carried by flow, we would rally and close the budget, month after month. Months became years, and the momentum just kept on growing.

Flow, as explained earlier, enables the best output and facilitates peak performances. Everything just clicks. If obstacles are met, they are overcome by solutions, melting away like popsicles under the sun. When an employee experiences FLOW@WORK, that same employee is experiencing a magical moment in time. Suddenly, work does not feel like work anymore. Work becomes an intense source of pleasure and joy. It brings contentment, growth and momentum. Some of the characteristics found in fully engaged, satisfied and happy employees are amplified performance, greater creativity, more access to intuition and an ever-increasing ability to engage in deep learning. To identify and then cultivate the conditions that enable those employees to experience flow rests as much with leadership and the company's culture as it does with the individual.

According to Daniel Goleman, 'In flow, we channel positive feelings in an energized pursuit of the task at hand. Our focus is undistracted, and we feel a spontaneous joy, even rapture. There's a quality of effortlessness to our work. This state of maximum cognitive efficiency leads to increased productivity.' When an employee is emotionally invested in the work, loves what he or she does, experts refer to this principle as being an *intrinsic motivation*. This is that same intrinsic motivation that moved me to come back to the workforce after the birth of our twins and to become an agent of change and bring FLOW@WORK.

Figure 14.1 Commitment Sparks FLOW@WORK

As a flow leader, your commitment to help your *people* get as close to their maximum *flow* state as possible is what will make or break the process (Figure 14.1). And as such, it is essential that you maintain the momentum of this initiative. This ensures it becomes not only top of mind but also a top business priority.

Part II

Key Takeaways

10 **Bringing *Purpose* to the Workplace**

- Transform the workplace by transitioning from top-down to horizontal leadership by nurturing vulnerability and showing true colours.
- Ignite *purpose* in your *people* by instilling a feeling of fulfilment and appreciation for the impact of their work.

FlowBite: *Purpose-driven work is a source of energy that fuels passion, perseverance, and FLOW@WORK.*

11 **What Does Purpose Mean for Your People?**

- Design an organization with *purpose* in helping your *people* find and see how their purpose is contributing towards the purpose of the organization.
- Align individual values with company values to foster a purposeful work environment and ensure long-term engagement.
- Ignite passion by encouraging your *people* to identify and integrate their passions at work, enhancing motivation and innovation.

FlowBite: *Unite through purpose.*

12 **What Is FLOW@WORK?**

- Foster *flow* by creating an environment where your *people* can fully immerse in their tasks, enhancing focus, creativity and productivity.
- Cultivate FLOW@WORK by developing a mindset that encourages *flow* to drive employee engagement and team efficiency.

FlowBite: *Bring FLOW@WORK to boost focus and efficiency.*

13 **Design Your FLOW@WORK Workshop Series**

- Identify and nurture each team member's intrinsic motivations and professional ambitions to connect their purpose with meaningful work.
- Facilitate authentic connections in using tools like the 'blazon exercise' and flow assessments to build trust, transparency and collaboration within teams.
- Cultivate team synergy by implementing workshops and structured activities to break down silos, align team goals and foster a unified, purpose-driven culture.

FlowBite: *Lead with purpose; inspire with flow.*

14 **It All Starts with You as Leaders**

- Engage in the FLOW@WORK journey to harness your team potential, fostering an environment of creativity, productivity and purpose by focusing on mindset and authentic growth.
- As a flow leader, your dedication is crucial to maintaining momentum, ensuring that the principles of *flow* drive exponential growth in terms of *people* and *performance and* become a top business priority.

FlowBite: *Unlock your team's potential with FLOW@WORK, where passion and purpose drive peak performance.*

Part III

Performance

15

Time for a New Set of KPIs

Performance and *flow* are intertwined concepts. *Flow* is a state of high performance, and high-performance tasks often trigger the *flow* state.

When employees experience a sense of competence and achievement, they are more likely to enter *flow*. It is the zone of *natural excellence* and your third 'P', positioned at the top corner of the *flow leadership* triangle. It signifies the goal of enhanced organizational performance – its output. And it is met when *people* and *purpose* align seamlessly.

In *flow leadership*, the foundation for achieving optimal performance lies in understanding and leveraging the first two P's – *people and purpose*. They serve as the bedrock upon which effective leadership is built. When leaders invest time and effort in getting to know their team members – their strengths, weaknesses, aspirations and motivations – they foster an environment of trust, collaboration and empowerment.

Similarly, clarifying the purpose behind tasks and projects provides direction and meaning to the work undertaken by individuals and teams. By aligning – *people* with *purpose*, leaders create a pathway for their teams to reach a state of *natural excellence*, where skills are matched to the right level of challenge. In return, this leads to enhanced performance and productivity as explored in Part II of this book.

Think of performance as the outcome of your 'matchmaking' skill. It is about combining your people's unique capabilities with a shared sense of purpose and matching the skillset to the 'right' level of challenge. Matching skills involves understanding the unique capabilities and proficiencies of each team member and aligning them with tasks and challenges that correspond to their abilities.

This process requires a deep understanding of everyone's strengths, weaknesses and areas for growth. To build high-performing teams, leaders need to understand the skills of their team members. They can do this by observing their performance, giving feedback and keeping communication lines open (Figure 15.1).

Figure 15.1 Performance Through Skill Matching

To raise the level of self-awareness in a team, it is suggested to prompt the people to assess their own soft skills. This can be done utilizing self-assessment tools or surveys. This fundamental process aids the team members in pinpointing their strengths and areas for skill enhancement. It brings to awareness the essence of who they are in the workplace and where some of the work could be done.

Among the arsenal of assessment tools available, we find Patrick Lencioni's 6 Types of Working Genius and the Head & Heart Leader Scale. Additionally, it may be worth considering leveraging the Gallup StrengthsFinder assessment, the Myers-Briggs Type Indicator (MBTI), DiSC assessments and the VIA Character Strengths survey.

These assessment tools furnish leaders and employees with invaluable insights, empowering them to identify and capitalize on their strengths and lesser strengths. This, in turn, facilitates the optimization of team performance and cultivates a conducive work environment. Moreover, these tools serve as indispensable aids in aligning individual skills with overarching business objectives.

By knowing your people and understanding their strengths, weaknesses and motivations, leaders can then match them to tasks and projects that provide an appropriate level of challenge. This requires careful consideration of the complexity, scope and requirements of each assignment.

Tasks that are too simple may lead to boredom and disengagement, while those that are overly complex may result in frustration and stress. For example, if a task is too easy for an individual, they may become bored and disengaged, resulting in subpar performance. On the other hand, if a task is too difficult and exceeds an individual's skill level, they may feel overwhelmed and stressed, leading to errors and inefficiencies.

By finding the right balance between skills and challenges, leaders create that zone of *natural excellence*, where individuals are working on tasks that challenge them just enough to engage their skills fully without overwhelming them (Figure 15.2). In this zone, individuals can fully leverage their skills and expertise to overcome obstacles and achieve their goals. They experience a sense of accomplishment and fulfilment as they work on tasks that align with their abilities and interests. In this state, people will feel at their best, be at their best and produce their best work. This is the Holy Grail and when FLOW@WORK is met.

Ultimately, the process of matching skills involves a combination of understanding individual strengths, assessing task requirements and creating opportunities for growth and development. When executed effectively,

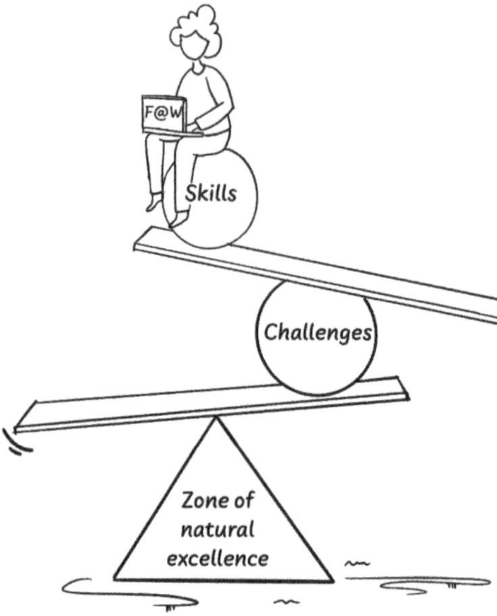

Figure 15.2 The Balance of Excellence: Where Skills and Challenges Meet

it enables leaders to harness the full potential of their team members and drive performance to new heights.

This is how you can empower your people to perform at their best. When people leverage their zone of *natural excellence*, they embrace their unique talents and produce their best work. And when, in addition, individuals see the direct link between their effort and the greater purpose, they are motivated to perform at their best. People love to make a difference and when they see their impact, they feel like they matter. This feeling gives them wings and thirst to succeed.

In the end, as a leader, this book may have triggered a desire to bring FLOW@WORK or at least some elements of it. If this is the case, it is fantastic, and I am grateful and honoured by your trust. Let me, however, warn you that without changing your outlook on what performance means, your efforts will not pay off as they should. And you will not succeed as you should. This is because it all starts with changing the way you look at key performances indicators (KPIs).

In today's business landscape, KPIs often revolve around traditional metrics such as sales targets, revenue growth and operational efficiency. While these metrics provide valuable insights into the success of a business, they tend to focus on quantitative measures that mainly serve the interests of the system rather than the people within it.

However, in an ideal scenario, KPIs should evolve to prioritize metrics that capture how people are doing. These new KPIs are designed to maximize individual potential and foster a culture of engagement and fulfilment within the organization. Metrics such as the flow level, which measures the degree of flow experienced by team members, and the strengths-alignment index, which evaluates the alignment between individuals' strengths and their roles, could be a starting point.

While traditional KPIs offer valuable insights into financial and operational performance, they often overlook the human element that drives success. People-centric KPIs complement traditional metrics by providing a deeper understanding of the organization's culture, employee well-being and capacity for innovation. By incorporating both sets of KPIs, organizations can achieve a more balanced and holistic view of their performance.

It is important to recognize that traditional and people-centric KPIs are not mutually exclusive. Instead, they should coexist harmoniously within an organization's performance management framework. By leveraging both types of metrics, leaders gain a comprehensive understanding of their organization's strengths, weaknesses and opportunities for improvement. This holistic view enables them to make more informed decisions and take strategic actions that drive sustainable growth and success.

Ultimately, the integration of people-centric KPIs alongside traditional metrics empowers organizations to cultivate a culture of continuous improvement, employee empowerment and organizational resilience. By embracing this holistic approach to performance measurement, organizations can unlock new levels of success while nurturing their most valuable asset – their *people*. This approach enables leaders to unlock the full potential of their teams and achieve sustainable success in today's competitive business environment.

Without this fundamental shift, everything else will simply be a waste of time. KPIs, or any performance management programmes, are often just another check-mark exercise usually serving the system. And it is now on you as leaders to challenge this reality and introduce a new paradigm. Some of your KPIs should be about your people, and solely about your people. Remember, as the *flow* leader that you are, 'dare to care' and performance will follow.

So let us pause for a moment and reflect on your organization's approach to supporting your team's well-being and performance. Consider the following questions:

Are there any KPIs in your organization that prioritize the well-being and growth of your team members?
If so, what are these KPIs?
How are they incorporated into your organization's processes?
Have these KPIs positively impacted your team members and the overall work environment? If so, how?

Are these KPIs integrated into your organization's performance evaluation cycle, or are they treated separately?
How does your organization actively engage with these KPIs to ensure they are effective?
What specific effects do these KPIs have on the happiness and productivity of your people?
How do these KPIs contribute to creating a supportive and fulfilling work environment for your team?
If your organization does not currently utilize such KPIs, have you considered, as the leader that you are, introducing any for your teams?
If yes, what specific KPIs are you considering, and how do you anticipate they will benefit your team?

Additionally, reflect on whether you or your HR department conduct assessments about strengths and skills, for example, like those mentioned above.

If not, do you actively observe and communicate with your team members to understand their strengths and challenges?
Are you equipped with the necessary information and resources to support your team members in reaching their zone of 'natural excellence'?
Do you have a sense of your team members' level of engagement and satisfaction in their roles?
Are they operating within an environment that allows them to perform at their best?

Reflecting on these questions can offer valuable insights into how your organization cultivates a supportive and high-performing work culture, anchored in the appropriate KPIs framework. The best intentions can mean nothing if the wrong measurements are used. Setting up appropriate KPI logic makes the difference between just talking about people driving performance and really managing it.

In today's business world, companies mostly focus on performance. They really care about getting the work done efficiently and focus a lot on making sure everyone meets their goals. If someone does not do well, leaders often push them to do better. And even when people do meet their goals, they do not always get recognized. Many leaders just see it as part of the job – people are paid to do their work, right?

But here is the thing: taking a moment to say 'good job' can make a big difference. It boosts morale and makes people feel valued. Plus, it encourages them to keep doing their best. So, even though it might seem like just another task for leaders, showing appreciation can help the whole team succeed in the long run.

And how do they do it? By focusing on the first 'P' – *people*. By building strong relationships and fostering a sense of belonging, leaders create an environment where recognition and appreciation come naturally. This, combined with a clear sense of *purpose*, where team members understand the importance and impact of their work, forms the foundation for a high-performing team.

Yet, as we have seen, the 3Ps of the *flow leadership* triangle operate in a chronological sequence. This means that when the third 'P' is emphasized, there is a need to revisit the first 'P' – *people*, and shortly after the second 'P' – *purpose*. After all, just like any engine, whether small or large, requires maintenance and care, so do your people. It is vital to genuinely make them feel valued and appreciated. And while doing so, it is crucial to keep doing so with *purpose*. With this understanding in mind, let me share a personal story to illustrate this concept.

Imagine living in New York City, feeling lost and lonely. That was me. I wanted to try something new to heal my heart, so I decided on long-distance road cycling. But I had no clue where to start. Big bike shops were no help – they just wanted to sell me an expensive bike. Feeling lost, I wandered into a small shop near my apartment. There, I met a man who did not just see a customer; he saw someone in need of guidance and support. "Are you free tomorrow morning?" he asked. And just like that, my journey began.

At 6 a.m. the next day, I found myself at George Washington Bridge, unsure of what lay ahead. With a simple bike – not the fanciest, but one that would do the job – we set off for an 80-kilometre ride. It was exhilarating, but soon enough, exhaustion hit me like a ton of bricks. Ever heard of hitting a wall? Well, I hit it hard. All I had was a banana. Needless to say, my legs felt like jelly and refused to cooperate. But just when I thought I could not go on, a helping hand reached out to me.

The man leading the ride, an ex-pro cyclist, told me to take his wheel. I had no clue what that meant, but in that moment, I did not hesitate. I followed his lead, pushing myself beyond what I thought possible. Then, his wife handed me an energy gel – a lifesaver in that moment. As I struggled to keep up with the pace, she showed me kindness and support, just like her husband. When I faltered again, feeling like I could not go on, the leader did not leave me behind. Instead, he rode beside me, gently pushing me forward while never slowing down.

After the ride, back at the shop, the team welcomed me warmly. They did not just sell me a bike; they made me feel like part of a tribe. And in doing so, they enabled me to keep on track with the purpose of this all.

This experience resonated deeply with me, not just because it introduced me to the world of cycling but because it highlighted profound lessons in leadership and customer experience.

As a leader, the importance of being present in the moment for your team cannot be overstated. When you are there, not just physically but emotionally and mentally, you create a bond of trust and support that empowers your team to overcome challenges and achieve remarkable feats.

In the context of cycling, the moment I felt like giving up, it was not the prospect of a shiny new bike or the promise of glory that kept me going. It was the simple act of the shop owner riding alongside me, guiding me with a gentle hand on my back, that made all the difference. His unwavering support showed me that leadership is not just about giving orders from the sidelines; it is about being in the trenches with your team, experiencing their struggles first hand and offering a helping hand when they need it most.

Moreover, the significance of genuine customer experience cannot be overlooked. In today's fast-paced world, where transactions often feel impersonal and fleeting, the value of authentic connection cannot be overstated. The small shop where I found support did not just sell me a bike; they welcomed me into a community, offering guidance, encouragement and a sense of belonging. They not only made me a forever customer but also left a mark that went beyond business. They helped me heal my heart while riding on two wheels, reaching my purpose in the process.

And let me tell you, it was quite a surprise when I discovered that cycling was secretly sculpting my abs into something resembling a six-pack! Who knew that the bumpy roads and uphill battles would turn out to be the ultimate workout for my core? Sadly, fast-forward a few years, I had twins, and those abs are now just a memory. Turns out, raising twins is quite the workout on its own! And hey, maybe cycling was just preparing me for the wild ride of parenthood – I guess that is its true purpose!

Now shifting focus from personal anecdotes, let us explore the underlying reason for sharing this story. Drawing a parallel between leadership and customer experience, it becomes evident that both hinge on empathy, authenticity and a genuine desire to make a positive impact. Just as a leader's support can inspire a team to achieve greatness, a memorable customer experience can foster loyalty and advocacy that propels a business to success (Figure 15.3).

Figure 15.3 The Drive for Five

Ultimately, it all ties back to performance. Whether it is the performance of a team striving to reach new heights or the performance of a business aiming to delight its customers, the principles remain the same. By prioritizing genuine connection, empathy and support, leaders can unlock the full potential of their teams, while businesses can create meaningful experiences that resonate long after the transaction is complete.

In essence, leadership is not just about guiding others; it is about inspiring them to greatness through empathy and support. Similarly, customer experience is not just about making a sale; it is about forging meaningful connections that leave a lasting impression. When approached with sincerity and care, both leadership and customer experience become powerful tools for driving performance and achieving success in any endeavour.

Just as a cyclist's leader knows precisely when to hand over the next energy gel, so too must a leader be attuned to the challenges their team faces, offering support and guidance at precisely the right moment. For it is only by witnessing the unfolding journey and understanding the obstacles that the correct tools can be provided to ensure success.

Just like when cyclists need to take a break and regain their energy during a tough ride, leaders should also understand that their teams need time to rest and recover after reaching goals. So the next time your team achieves something great and you want to ask for more, consider giving them some time to catch their breath. While it is important to keep pushing for success, taking a moment to celebrate and appreciate their hard work is just as crucial. It is during these times that they can refill their energy levels and be ready for the next challenge.

Performance needs to be positioned differently. Because as it stands today, performance is often the only topic that a leader will spend time discussing with the team. Yet to concentrate on the output only is utopian. If you do not concentrate on the input, how can you understand what is in the way of reaching that performance your team is chasing? How can you refill your people's energy levels to give more? How will you know how to show up for your people? Often the system and its leaders suck their people dry. And when there is nothing else to squeeze, people become the problem. And we all know where this may lead.

Approaching KPIs and performance in a new light is a fantastic starting point. But it is not enough. Just as it was suggested earlier in the book to reposition training and coaching as enablers of performance, it is now time to extend that mindset to how performance is perceived.

Regardless of the type of KPIs chosen, they represent the outcomes that both the team and the leader are responsible for achieving. If they fail, it means that as a leader you have failed them. There might be some exceptions, like if someone is not ready for the challenge. But often, when targets are missed, it is both the team's and the leader's responsibility.

Now, imagine taking a step back and really understanding your team – what they need to succeed. By filling in the gaps and leading them effectively, their success becomes your success. You have worked together to make it happen, and that is what FLOW@WORK is all about. It is journey in co-accountability and co-creation. It is about boosting your team's performance by focusing on each person individually for the greater good of the team and using new ways to measure success (Figure 15.4).

Your people are the key to your success, so handle them with care and guide them to a state of *flow* and *natural excellence*. Those are the KPIs that will drive you toward the performance you aim for. This is the essence of the third 'P': *performance*. Embrace it, and watch your team thrive.

Figure 15.4 Climbing Together: Lifting Success to New Heights

16

The FLOW@WORK Equation

In the world of *flow leadership*, the 3Ps – *People, Purpose* and *Performance* – are key ingredients for success. It is about getting the right *people*, aligning them with a clear *purpose* and ensuring they perform at their best.

The question is: how do we bring these concepts together to create a truly dynamic workplace? Enter the FLOW@WORK equation used to illustrate the interplay between the 3Ps and their impact on organizational success.

$$\text{FLOW@WORK} = (\textit{people} \times \textit{purpose})/\textit{performance}$$

As a start, let us unpack this equation with real-world examples. Imagine a company facing a major project deadline. The team tasked with delivering the project consists of highly skilled individuals (*performance*) who are deeply committed to the organization's mission (*purpose*). However, despite their talent and dedication, they find themselves struggling to collaborate effectively and meet the project goals. This is where the element of *people* comes into play.

Recognizing the importance of team dynamics, the leader decides to focus on building a stronger sense of camaraderie and trust among team members. Through team-building activities, open communication channels and regular feedback sessions, the leader cultivates a supportive environment where team members feel valued, respected and empowered to contribute their best. As a result, the team's cohesion and collaboration improve significantly, leading to a boost in performance and ultimately project success (Figure 16.1).

Now, let us apply the FLOW@WORK equation to this scenario. The equation suggests that FLOW@WORK is influenced by the combination of the *people* and *purpose* aspects, divided by the level of *performance*.

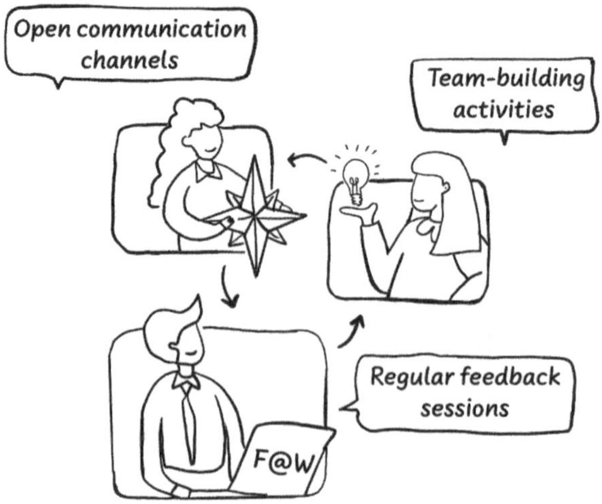

Figure 16.1 Importance of Creating a Supportive and Dynamic Workplace

In this case, the leader's efforts to strengthen team dynamics (*people*) and reinforce the organization's mission (*purpose*) contribute to a positive work environment where flow experiences are more likely to occur. However, the level of *performance* remains a crucial factor, ensuring that the team's skills and abilities align effectively with the challenges they face.

As the project progresses, the leader observes how the team members effortlessly collaborate, leveraging their diverse skills and perspectives to overcome obstacles and achieve their goals. This state not only enhances the team's performance but also fosters a culture of innovation and continuous improvement within the organization.

Now imagine a team of software developers working tirelessly on a project with a tight deadline. Each member is deeply engaged in their tasks, collaborating seamlessly with their colleagues and drawing upon their unique strengths and expertise. Despite the pressure, there is a sense of excitement and purpose in the air as they strive to create a product that will revolutionize the industry. This team embodies the essence of FLOW@WORK, where individuals are fully immersed in their work, driven by a shared purpose and achieving remarkable results.

Consider the story of Emily, a marketing manager at a global corporation. When she first joined the company, she felt disconnected from its mission and struggled to find meaning in her work. However, after attending a company-wide retreat focused on clarifying the organization's purpose and values, Emily experienced a profound shift in perspective. She realized that her role played a crucial part in advancing the company's mission of empowering communities and making a positive impact on society. Armed with this newfound clarity, Emily approached her tasks with renewed vigour and enthusiasm, leading to a noticeable improvement in her performance and overall job satisfaction.

To continue, let us look at a different scenario. Imagine a sales team struggling with unrealistic targets and mounting pressure from upper management. Despite their best efforts, team members find themselves constantly falling short of their goals. This leads them to feeling frustrated and demotivated. In this environment, the lack of alignment between the organization's expectations and the team's capabilities stifles creativity, innovation and productivity. Without a clear sense of purpose and support from leadership, the team struggles to find its footing and achieve a state of FLOW@WORK.

In contrast, consider the story of Sasha, a team leader at a rapidly growing startup. Recognizing the importance of fostering a culture of *flow*, Sasha takes proactive steps to empower his team and create an environment where they can thrive. He encourages open communication, values each team member's input and provides opportunities for growth and development. By aligning the team's efforts with the company's overarching purpose and celebrating their achievements along the way, Sasha cultivates a sense of belonging and fulfilment among his team members. As a result, they approach their work with renewed energy and enthusiasm, driving the company's success forward.

Figure 16.2 Unlocking the Power of FLOW@WORK

These stories illustrate how the principles of FLOW@WORK come to life in real-world scenarios. By prioritizing the well-being and engagement of *people*, aligning efforts with a compelling purpose and maintaining a relentless focus on performance, leaders can unlock the transformative power of *flow* and propel their organizations to new heights of success (Figure 16.2).

More concretely, let us break down this equation and understand how it drives success in organizations.

P1 (People):

People represent more than just individuals within the organization; they are the lifeblood of the company, driving its success. When team members feel valued, respected and supported in their roles, they are more likely to bring their full selves to work, fostering an environment ripe for flow experiences. This represents the impact of the team members' engagement, collaboration and emotional intelligence. The more engaged and emotionally connected the team members are, the greater their potential to experience *flow*.

P2 (Purpose):

This refers to the alignment of individual and team goals with the organization's purpose and mission. When team members understand and connect with the broader purpose of their work, it enhances their sense of meaning and purpose, leading to a higher likelihood of entering a state of *flow*. *Purpose* serves as a guiding light, illuminating the path forward and infusing every task and initiative with meaning and significance. When employees understand how their work contributes to the organization's larger objectives, they are more motivated, committed and invested in their roles, paving the way for enhanced performance and flow. However, purpose alone is not enough to cultivate FLOW@WORK; it must be complemented by performance, the third pillar of the equation.

P3 (Performance):

This factor accounts for the balance between the challenges presented by tasks and the team members' skill levels. The higher the performance and skill development, the more likely team members are to meet challenges effectively. Moreover, performance acts as a moderating force within the equation, ensuring that challenges are neither too overwhelming nor too trivial for team members to tackle effectively. By continually striving for performance excellence and fostering a culture of continuous improvement, leaders can empower their teams to reach new heights of productivity, creativity and innovation.

Figure 16.3 The FLOW@WORK Equation:

The division of (*people* × *purpose*) by *performance* in the FLOW@WORK equation serves a crucial purpose in balancing the elements of *flow* within an organization (Figure 16.3). By dividing the combined impact of *people* and *purpose* by *performance*, the equation ensures that the organization's resources, including its human capital and collective purpose, are effectively aligned with the level of performance required to achieve its goals. This division helps in optimizing resources and ensures that the organization's efforts are directed towards tasks and challenges that match its capabilities and objectives.

Performance acts as a moderating factor in the equation, ensuring that the level of challenge presented by tasks aligns appropriately with the skills and abilities of the individuals or teams involved. As seen earlier, if the performance level is too high relative to the capabilities of the people or the clarity of purpose, it may lead to feelings of overwhelm, stress or disengagement. Conversely, if performance exceeds expectations relative to people and purpose, it may signal underutilized potential or a lack of alignment with organizational objectives.

To sum up, the FLOW@WORK equation – *(people × purpose) / performance* – underscores the intricate interplay between these three components. It highlights the symbiotic relationship between engaged and purpose-driven individuals (*people*) and a clear alignment with the organization's purpose (*purpose*), both of which are essential for creating an environment conducive to *flow*.

In other words, this means that a strong alignment with the organization's purpose and a sense of meaning in work (*purpose*), combined with engaged, collaborative and emotionally connected team members (*people*), lead to higher potential for FLOW@WORK. However, FLOW@WORK is moderated by the level of *performance*, which indicates the extent to which the challenges faced match the team and team members' skills and abilities.

If the performance is low, it can hinder the likelihood of experiencing *flow*, even in a purposeful and people-centric environment. By fostering a positive and purpose-driven work environment (*people × purpose*) while maintaining a focus on performance excellence (divided by *performance*), flow leaders can create conditions that enhance the likelihood of FLOW@WORK.

In conclusion, FLOW@WORK represents the pinnacle of organizational success, where individuals thrive, teams flourish and the company achieves its fullest potential. By prioritizing the well-being and engagement of their *people*, aligning their efforts with a compelling *purpose*, and maintaining a relentless focus on *performance*, leaders can unlock the transformative power of FLOW@WORK.

17

The 3Ps Equilibrium Equation

To create a thriving work environment, it is essential to strike a balance on the 3Ps – *People, Purpose* and *Performance* – as we have seen earlier. In doing so, leaders can create a harmonious and high-performing work environment that values their people, pursues a meaningful purpose and achieves outstanding results.

In *flow leadership*, it is accepted that a people-centric approach should coexist with a clear sense of purpose and performance expectations. And as a flow leader, you should aim to communicate the organization's purpose and vision to your teams to ensure everyone is aligned with the broader mission. Remember to set clear performance goals and provide regular feedback to help your people understand their progress and areas for improvement. Try to foster a culture of empathy and support while also encouraging a strong focus on achieving results and excellence. And last but not least, encourage open dialogue and collaboration while ensuring that decisions and actions are aligned with the organization's purpose and strategic objectives. A big task but you have what it takes to do it. Plant the seed of change and witness your people bloom.

Now, as seen in the previous chapter, the FLOW@WORK equation – (*people* × *purpose*) / *performance* – highlights the interdependence of the 3Ps – *People, Purpose* and *Performance*. In essence, it suggests that achieving a state of *flow* in the workplace requires a balance between these factors.

The FLOW@WORK equation emphasizes the need for synergy between – *People, Purpose* and *Performance* – to achieve *flow*. It suggests that when these elements are in harmony, individuals and teams are more likely to experience a state of *flow*, characterized by deep engagement, creativity and productivity.

In the FLOW@WORK equation, *performance* is used as a divisor because it represents the balance between the challenges presented by tasks and the skill levels of individuals or teams. This division emphasizes the importance of matching task challenges with skill levels to facilitate a state of *flow*.

To strike a balance between the 3Ps – *People, Purpose* and *Performance* – in a workplace, we can create an equation that highlights their interdependence. Let us call this equation 'the 3Ps equilibrium equation'.

The 3Ps equilibrium equation = *people* + *purpose* + *performance*

The 3Ps equilibrium equation, which sums up to *people* + *purpose* + *performance*, underscores the importance of each element. It acknowledges that while these elements interact to facilitate *flow*, they also need to be individually nurtured and maintained for optimal performance.

It reminds us that each element – *People, Purpose* and *Performance* – plays a distinct role in shaping the work environment and organizational culture. And it emphasizes the importance of ensuring balance and alignment across all three dimensions to foster a healthy and thriving workplace.

This balance ensures that the well-being and engagement of employees (*people*) are supported, aligned with a clear and meaningful organizational purpose (*purpose*), and channelled towards high levels of performance and productivity (*performance*).

Unlike the FLOW@WORK equation, the equilibrium equation does not use *performance* as a denominator because it aims to illustrate the balance between – *people, purpose* and *performance* – in a holistic manner. Instead of treating *performance* as a separate factor, the equilibrium equation considers it as an integral part of the overall equilibrium among the 3Ps.

By including *performance* as a separate factor in the equilibrium equation, it could potentially overshadow the interconnectedness of – *people* and *purpose* with *performance*. Thus, *performance* is not treated as a denominator in the equilibrium equation to maintain a focus on the holistic balance among the three components.

Both equations together provide a comprehensive framework for understanding and optimizing the dynamics of the workplace. By focusing on achieving equilibrium across the 3Ps while also fostering synergy between them, leaders can create an environment that nurtures *flow*, fosters employee well-being and drives organizational success.

- P1 *people*: This represents the focus on creating a people-centric work environment that emphasizes employee well-being, engagement and collaboration.
- P2 *purpose*: This factor reflects the organization's clear sense of purpose, mission and values that guide the actions and goals of the employees.
- P3 *performance*: This component signifies the emphasis on achieving high levels of performance, productivity and results in alignment with the organization's purpose.

By giving due attention to *People, Purpose* and *Performance*, leaders can foster a work environment that promotes employee well-being, meaningful contributions and outstanding results. Striking this equilibrium is vital for creating a thriving and successful organization that excels in both the human and business aspects of its operations.

In the world of organizations, finding balance is crucial for long-term success. But sometimes, things get out of balance. Imagine focusing too much on one thing and ignoring the rest. That is where the imbalance equations come in. These equations show us what happens when we put too much emphasis on one of the 3Ps – *people, purpose or performance* – and not enough on the others. By exploring these imbalances, we can see how they affect employees, company culture and overall performance. Let us dive in and see why it is important to keep – *People, Purpose* and *Performance* – in harmony (Figure 17.1).

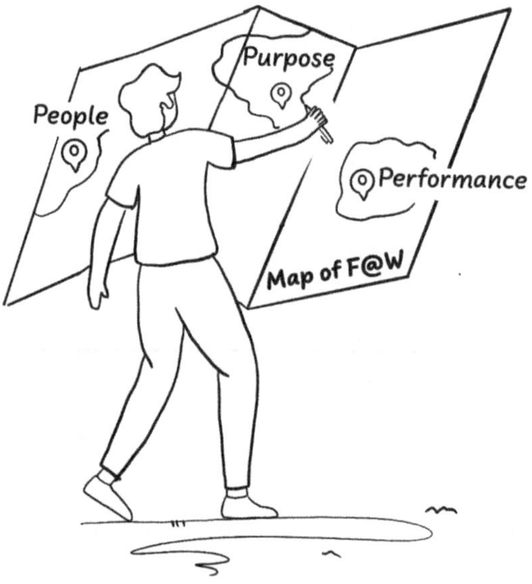

Figure 17.1 Mapping the 3Ps: A Compass for Balanced Success

$$\text{People imbalance equation} = (2 \times \textit{people}) + \textit{purpose} + \textit{performance}$$

This equation magnifies the importance of *people* by doubling its weight, overshadowing the significance of *purpose* and *performance*. It reflects a scenario where the organization excessively focuses on employee well-being and satisfaction, neglecting clear goals and performance expectations.

- P1 *people* (2 × *people*): In this imbalance equation, the focus on people is magnified by multiplying it by two. This indicates an excessive emphasis on creating a people-centric work environment, possibly to the detriment of other important aspects.
- P2 *purpose*: This factor remains unchanged, representing the organization's clear sense of purpose and mission.
- P3 *performance*: This component also remains unchanged, signifying the focus on achieving high levels of performance and results.

Let us take an example to better grasp the concept. Think of a tech startup where the CEO prioritizes employee perks and benefits to create a fun and relaxed work environment. While the team enjoys free meals, game rooms and flexible hours, the lack of clear goals and performance metrics leads to confusion and inefficiency. Despite high employee satisfaction, the company struggles to meet its targets and falls behind competitors.

As a result of the imbalance equation, the tech startup may experience several challenges. Without clear objectives and performance metrics, employees lack direction and motivation, leading to inefficiency and decreased productivity. Additionally, the lack of accountability and goal alignment hinders collaboration and teamwork, further exacerbating the company's performance issues. Ultimately, the imbalance between – *people*, *purpose* and *performance* – will negatively impact the organization's competitiveness and long-term sustainability.

To address the imbalance and restore equilibrium, the tech startup could take several steps. First, the company should revisit its organizational goals and clearly define performance metrics aligned with its mission and objectives. This would involve emphasizing the importance of all 3Ps – *People, Purpose* and *Performance* – in driving the company forward. Leadership should communicate these goals effectively to employees, highlighting the significance of each aspect in achieving overall success.

Additionally, the organization should implement performance management systems and regular feedback mechanisms to track progress and hold employees accountable for results. This would involve focusing on performance, ensuring that individuals understand their roles and responsibilities in contributing to the company's objectives. By providing clear expectations and feedback, employees can better understand how their efforts align with the organization's purpose and mission.

Furthermore, the company should introduce a measure linked directly to its purpose. For example, if the startup's purpose is to improve environmental sustainability, a relevant measure could be the reduction of carbon emissions or the adoption of eco-friendly practices in daily operations. By incorporating purpose-driven metrics into performance evaluations, employees are incentivized to contribute to the organization's broader mission while also fulfilling their individual responsibilities.

While maintaining a focus on employee well-being (*people*), the company should ensure that perks and benefits are balanced with performance expectations. This would involve re-evaluating the current emphasis on employee satisfaction and considering how it can be integrated with performance-driven initiatives. For example, the company could offer incentives tied to specific performance goals or invest in training and development programmes to enhance employee skills and capabilities.

By fostering a culture that values both employee satisfaction and performance excellence, the startup can create a more sustainable and successful work environment. This balanced approach would enable the organization to leverage the strengths of its workforce while ensuring alignment with its strategic objectives. Ultimately, by restoring equilibrium among the 3Ps – *People, Purpose* and *Performance* – the tech startup can position itself for long-term success and growth in the competitive market landscape.

In general, one of the possible outcomes of such imbalances is for the organization to suffer from a high employee engagement but a lack of direction. An excessive focus on *people* without a balanced emphasis on *purpose* and *performance* will result in employees lacking clarity regarding their contributions to the organization's mission. Employees may feel disconnected from the organization's goals and objectives, leading to a loss of motivation. In addition, while prioritizing employee well-being is essential, an extreme focus on people may result in a lack of focus on achieving tangible outcomes and meeting performance goals.

With an imbalanced equation, there is a risk of overlooking performance expectations and not holding employees accountable for achieving desired results. Without clear performance expectations and goals, employees may lack the drive to excel in their roles. A lack of focus on performance may cause the organization to miss opportunities for growth and improvement. And without continuous feedback and goal setting, employees may not reach their full potential (Figure 17.2).

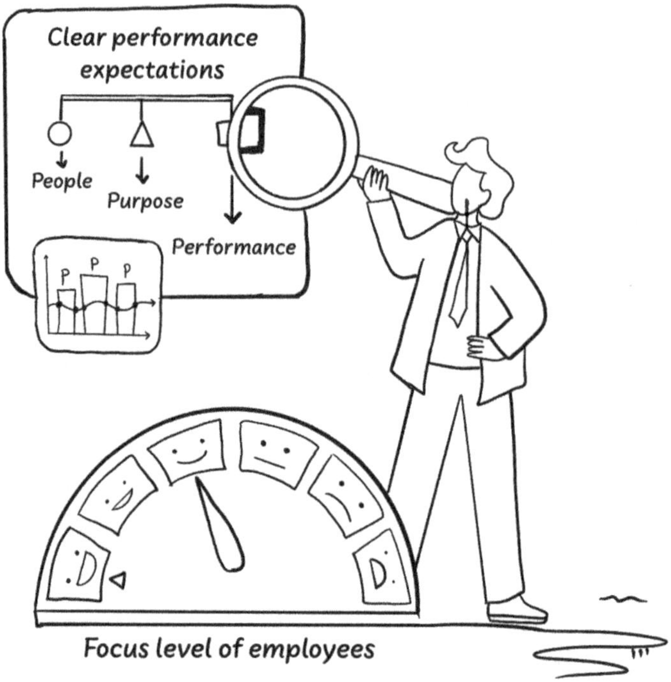

Figure 17.2 Mastering the Art of Balance: Leading with *People, Purpose* and *Performance*

While caring for employees is essential, an exclusive focus on people without considering performance and purpose on the same level of importance may lead to burnout if the organization fails to set boundaries and manage workload effectively. Lastly, it may generate a misalignment between individual and team goals and the broader organizational purpose, resulting in a fragmented approach to work. The famous silos dilemma that is present in so many companies. The 'imbalance equation' illustrates the potential consequences of an excessive emphasis on one of the 3Ps, in this example on the first P – *people*.

While it is essential to prioritize people and their well-being, leaders must strike a balanced approach that encompasses all three aspects of the 3Ps – *People, Purpose* and *Performance*. Such an approach will help create a successful and fulfilling work environment. Achieving a harmonious balance will empower employees to contribute meaningfully to the organization's purpose while also fostering a high-performance culture that drives results.

$$\text{Purpose imbalance equation}: \textit{people} + (2 \times \textit{purpose}) + \textit{performance}$$

This equation overemphasizes *purpose* by doubling its weight, minimizing the importance of *people* and *performance*. It illustrates a scenario where the organization is solely focused on its mission and goals, disregarding employee well-being and engagement.

In this scenario, the equation exaggerates the focus on *purpose* by doubling its weight, while underemphasizing the importance of *people* and *performance*.

In the following example, it reflects a situation where a luxury goods service provider overly prioritizes brand image, exclusivity and prestige, neglecting the needs of its employees and failing to deliver on performance metrics.

Picture a luxury hotel chain aiming to position itself as the epitome of elegance and sophistication, heavily investing in lavish decor, extravagant amenities and elite clientele. The company devotes significant resources to crafting a prestigious brand image and maintaining an aura of exclusivity. However, this singular focus on *purpose* comes at the expense of employee satisfaction and operational efficiency.

As a result, hotel staff may feel undervalued and overworked, leading to high turnover rates and a lack of morale among frontline employees. Despite the luxurious ambiance and upscale clientele, service quality may suffer due to disengaged or demotivated staff, resulting in negative guest experiences and declining customer satisfaction ratings.

To regain balance across the 3Ps – *People, Purpose* and *Performance* – the luxury hotel chain should implement strategic interventions aimed at aligning organizational goals with employee well-being and operational excellence.

Firstly, the company should prioritize initiatives that enhance employee engagement such as staff recognition programmes, professional development opportunities and work–life balance initiatives. By investing in the well-being and satisfaction of its workforce, the hotel can foster a positive workplace culture and improve staff retention rates.

Secondly, the organization should reassess its brand purpose and values to ensure alignment with both employee and customer expectations. Rather than solely focusing on luxury and exclusivity, the hotel should emphasize delivering exceptional service experiences rooted in genuine hospitality and personalized attention.

Lastly, the company should establish performance metrics that measure both customer satisfaction and employee effectiveness. This could involve implementing service standards and performance benchmarks that reflect the organization's commitment to both luxury and operational efficiency.

By addressing the imbalance between *purpose* and the other two Ps, the luxury hotel chain can create a more holistic approach to service delivery, enhancing both employee engagement and customer satisfaction. This balanced strategy will enable the organization to achieve its overarching goals while maintaining a competitive edge in the luxury hospitality industry.

Furthermore, embracing the concept of CX = EX (customer experience equals employee experience) as seen in Part I of this book, is crucial. Recognizing that the experience of employees directly impacts the experience of customers reinforces the need to prioritize both aspects equally. When employees feel valued, supported and engaged, they are more likely to deliver exceptional service experiences, ultimately enhancing overall customer satisfaction and loyalty. Thus, by aligning – *People, Purpose* and *Performance* – the luxury hotel chain can create a virtuous cycle where positive employee experiences translate into exceptional customer experiences, driving long-term success and profitability.

$$\text{Performance imbalance equation}: people + purpose + (2 \times performance)$$

This equation exaggerates the importance of *performance* by doubling its weight, while neglecting the significance of *people* and *purpose*. It portrays a scenario where the organization prioritizes short-term results over employee well-being and alignment with the company's mission.

As an example, let us look at a sales-driven company where the management sets aggressive sales targets and commission structures to incentivize performance. While the sales team consistently meets or exceeds their quotas, the intense pressure may lead to a toxic work environment marked by internal competition and distrust. Despite achieving financial success in the short term, the company will struggle with employee turnover and reputation damage in the long run.

The aggressive sales-driven culture created by the management may have several detrimental consequences for the organization. Firstly, while the sales team may have achieved their targets in the short term, the intense pressure to meet quotas fostered a toxic work environment characterized by internal competition, mistrust and burnout. This resulted in heightened stress levels among employees, leading to decreased morale, job dissatisfaction and ultimately, high turnover rates.

Additionally, the focus solely on sales targets and financial incentives overlooked the holistic well-being of employees. As a result, the company experienced reputation damage due to negative word of mouth from disgruntled employees and poor reviews from dissatisfied customers. The toxic work culture not only affected employee retention but also impacted customer satisfaction and loyalty, ultimately undermining the company's long-term success and profitability.

To address the imbalance and mitigate the negative consequences of the sales-driven culture, this company should implement strategic measures that prioritize the well-being of its employees while maintaining performance excellence (Figure 17.3).

Figure 17.3 Nurture Growth: Energize Your Team, Cultivate Their Values

Firstly, the organization should prioritize initiatives aimed at improving employee well-being and fostering a supportive work culture. This could involve providing regular opportunities for open communication, feedback and recognition. Additionally, implementing stress management programmes, work–life balance initiatives and employee assistance programmes can support the mental and emotional health of employees.

Secondly, the company should redefine its purpose beyond solely achieving sales targets and financial success. By emphasizing a broader mission centred around customer satisfaction, innovation and social responsibility, the company can align its goals with the values and aspirations of its employees. This shift in purpose can create a sense of meaning and fulfilment among employees, driving engagement and motivation.

Lastly, while maintaining performance excellence is important, the company should reassess its approach to goal setting and performance evaluation. Instead of solely focusing on sales quotas, the organization should adopt a more balanced approach that considers both quantitative metrics and qualitative indicators of success. This could involve incorporating customer feedback, employee engagement surveys and team collaboration metrics into performance evaluations to ensure a more holistic assessment of performance.

By prioritizing the well-being of its employees, redefining its purpose and adopting a more balanced approach to performance management, the company can create a healthier and more sustainable work culture. This balanced strategy will not only improve employee morale and retention but also enhance customer satisfaction, reputation and long-term business success.

In the world of leadership, achieving FLOW@WORK – a state where creativity, productivity and fulfilment converge – is paramount. *Flow leadership* involves keeping the balance between – *People, Purpose* and *Performance* – in perfect equilibrium.

At the heart of it, a leader must focus on supporting their people, clarifying the organization's goals and refining how things get done to facilitate FLOW@WORK. It is like being a steady hand on the wheel, guiding the ship through choppy waters while maintaining the rhythm of flow.

Success is not just about making money; it is about making a positive impact and leaving a legacy through *flow leadership*. A great leader understands this and works tirelessly to maintain the right balance, fostering an environment where FLOW@WORK thrives (Figure 17.4).

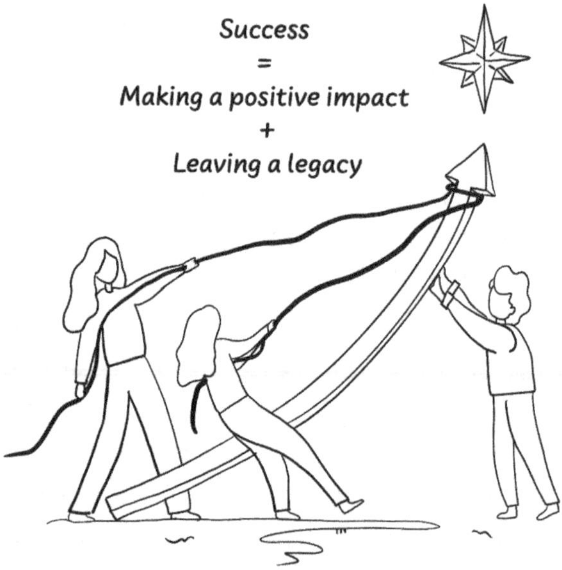

Figure 17.4 Redefining Success: Building a Legacy through *Flow Leadership*

In the end, the mark of a truly exceptional leader is not their title or their authority – it is their ability to keep things in *harmony*, even when faced with challenges. It is about finding that sweet spot where everyone thrives, and the business flourishes under the guiding principles of *flow leadership*.

18

Unpacking the Science

Research Foundations of FLOW@WORK and its Equilibrium Equations

To assess the 3Ps – *People, Purpose* and *Performance* – in your company, at an individual and collective level is essential. Such data will help call out what needs to be done, take the relevant decisions and make the required adjustments to reach FLOW@WORK.

Each of the 3Ps has a series of questions that the participants will need to answer. And the outcome of this assessment will illustrate if the 3Ps are in balance or if there is an imbalance skewed towards one of the 3Ps.

This questionnaire aims to gather feedback from your *people* about their experiences within the organization, focusing on the 3Ps – *People, Purpose* and *Performance*.

Your people's feedback through this questionnaire will help you gain valuable insights into their experiences within the organization across the 3Ps. Their input will enable you as the great leader that you are to identify areas for improvement and implement strategies to enhance their workplace environment.

Building on the insights gathered through this assessment, the aim of this chapter is to delve deeper into the evaluation and refinement of models that underpin FLOW@WORK. This index captures the dynamic interplay of *People, Purpose* and *Performance*, forming the foundation of a workplace environment that fosters engagement, satisfaction and productivity. By bridging practical observations with robust research, this chapter seeks to solidify the framework and guide its application in enhancing organizational success.

The research commenced with a pilot study involving a sample of (N = 60), which established foundational relationships among *People, Purpose* and *Performance* and provided an initial validation of the FLOW@WORK framework. Building on the insights and limitations of this initial phase, a second, more comprehensive study was conducted with an expanded sample of (N = 201) to confirm these relationships, explore potential refinements to the framework and ensure robustness across a broader range of workplace contexts.

The FLOW@WORK framework stems from recognizing that successful organizations must go beyond traditional productivity measures. Instead, they must balance between the following 3Ps:

- *People*: The social and emotional aspects of work, including personal needs, team dynamics, engagement and cohesion.
- *Purpose*: Alignment with organizational mission and the sense of meaning that drives motivation.
- *Performance*: The effective match between team skills and task challenges, ensuring that productivity is achieved without overwhelming or under-stimulating employees.

Across both studies, multiple mathematical models were explored to capture the nuanced interactions among these factors. These models emphasize different aspects of the *people-purpose-performance* relationship. The analysis employed a range of methods, including correlation analysis, regression models, reliability testing and confirmatory factor analysis alongside the introduction of alternative equations such as the 3Ps equilibrium equation and other formulas. Each method provided insights into the unique and combined impacts of the three key dimensions of leadership within varying organizational contexts.

Initial findings from the pilot study revealed that *people* and *performance* play central roles in driving FLOW@WORK, with *purpose* acting as a supportive factor. The second study confirmed these findings while identifying stronger correlations and regression models involving *purpose*, suggesting an enhanced role in linking team cohesion and productivity. Additionally, the reliability of the measures improved across studies. In the second study, we also explored a multidimensional *people* construct with seven dimensions. The aim of exploring this model was to investigate how each facet contributed to *people* and overall FLOW@WORK.

Ultimately, this report delivers a flexible framework for understanding flow in diverse workplace settings. By comparing findings across the pilot and second study, actionable insights are provided to help organizations optimize engagement and productivity, creating environments where employees thrive and achieve sustained high performance.

Preliminary Data Analysis

Correlations

In the pilot study, the correlation analysis between *People, Purpose* and *Performance* were as follows (see Figure 18.1):

- ***People*** **and** ***performance***: Strong positive correlation ($r = 0.75$), indicating that team dynamics are closely linked to productivity.
- ***People*** **and** ***purpose***: Moderate positive correlation ($r = 0.58$), suggesting that team cohesion enhances employees' alignment with organizational mission.
- ***Purpose*** **and** ***performance***: Moderate correlation ($r = 0.52$), showing that mission alignment supports productivity but is not a dominant driver.

These correlations suggest that *people* and *performance* play central roles in driving workflow, while *purpose* is a supportive, secondary factor.

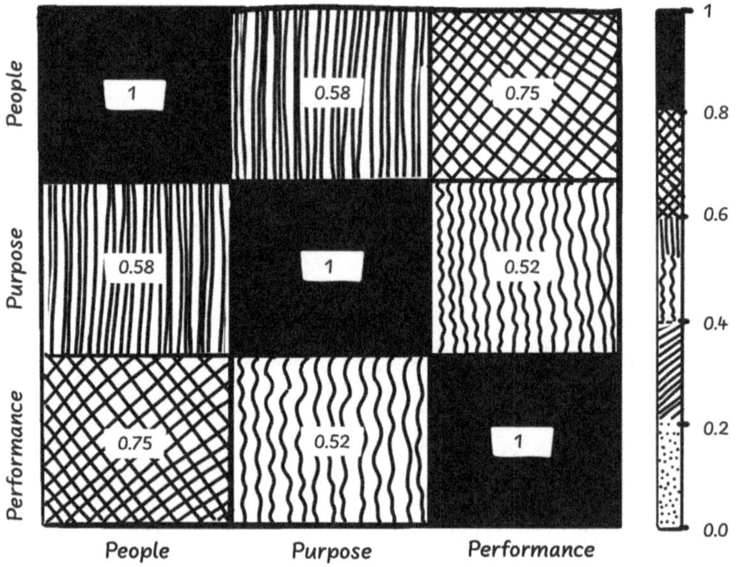

Figure 18.1 Correlation heat map for pilot study: *People*, *Purpose* and *Performance*

We repeated the same correlation analysis in the second study. The outcome was as follows:

- ***People*** **and** ***performance***: Strong positive correlation (r = 0.78), indicating that team dynamics are closely linked to productivity.
- ***People*** **and** ***purpose***: Moderate positive correlation (r = 0.70), suggesting that team cohesion enhances employees' alignment with organizational mission.
- ***Purpose*** **and** ***performance***: Moderate correlation (r = 0.70), showing that mission alignment supports productivity but is not a dominant driver.

The correlations confirmed the associations between the three constructs as in study one. However, *purpose* had stronger correlations with both *people* and *performance* in this study (see Figure 18.2).

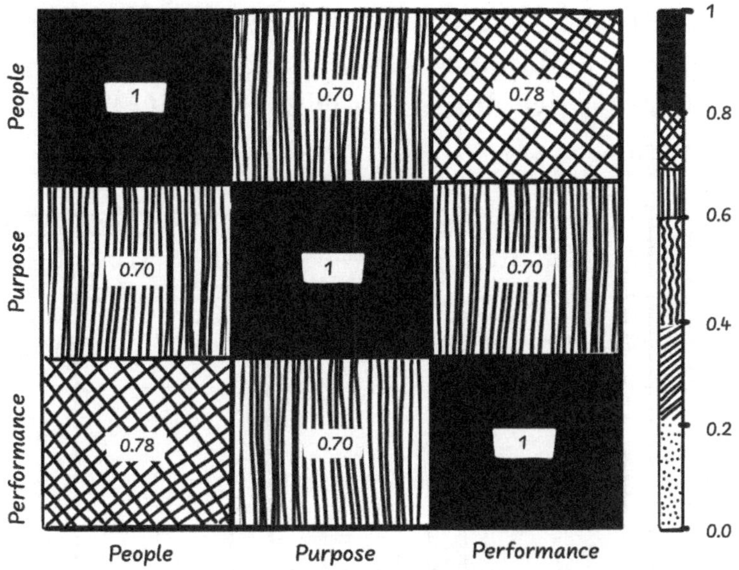

Figure 18.2 Correlation heat map for second study: *People, Purpose* and *Performance*

Scale Reliability Analysis

In both study one and two, three main scales – *People, Purpose* and *Performance* – were computed and assessed for reliability using Cronbach's alpha, a metric that evaluates the internal consistency of items within each scale. Reliability is essential in survey-based research as it ensures that the scales consistently measure their intended constructs, providing confidence in the stability and interpretability of the results.

Cronbach's alpha values above 0.70 indicate good internal consistency. The result for each scale in the pilot study was as follows:

- *People* ($\alpha = 0.87$)
- *Purpose* ($\alpha = 0.88$)
- *Performance* ($\alpha = 0.82$)

All three scales exceeded the recommended threshold (see Figure 18.3), indicating that each scale reliably captures its respective dimension within the FLOW@WORK framework.

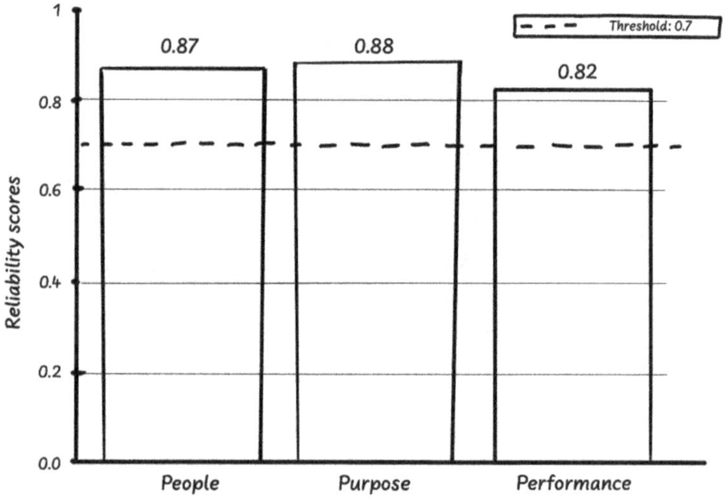

Figure 18.3 Reliability Scores by Variable (Pilot Study)

The same step was repeated in the second study (N = 201). The reliabilities were as follows (see Figure 18.4):

- *People* ($\alpha = 0.88$)
- *Purpose* ($\alpha = 0.88$)
- *Performance* ($\alpha = 0.87$)

The high reliabilities scores in both studies reinforce the validity of subsequent analyses, as they confirm that each variable is consistently measured across respondents.

Regression Analysis: Predicting *Performance* from *People* and *Purpose*

To investigate how *people* and *purpose* influence *performance*, we conducted regression analyses as part of the

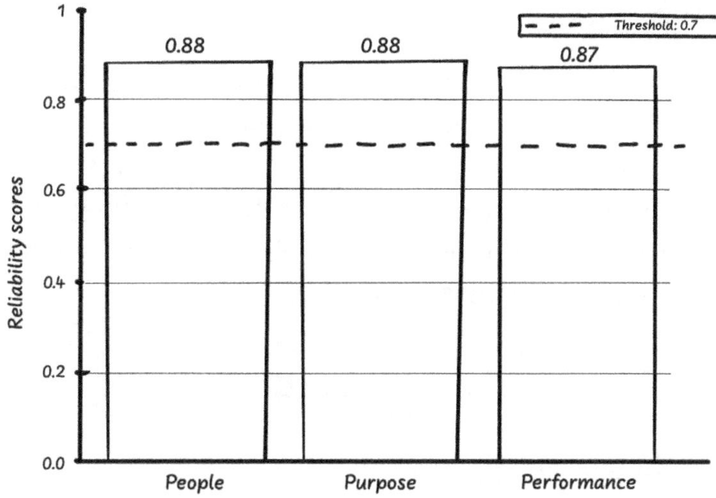

Figure 18.4 Reliability Scores by Variable (Second Study)

FLOW@WORK framework. These analyses aimed to evaluate the unique and combined contributions of these factors to workplace productivity. *Performance* was used as the dependent variable, with *people* and *purpose* as predictors.

Pilot Study Results: Combined and Solo Models

In the pilot study, both a combined model (*people* and *purpose* as predictors) and a solo model (*purpose* as the sole predictor) were tested to identify the impact of each factor.

People

In the combined model, *people* demonstrated a standardized coefficient of **0.625**, which was statistically significant ($p < 0.001$). This result highlights *people*'s strong and central role in predicting *performance*, suggesting that team dynamics, engagement and cohesion are pivotal to productivity.

Purpose

Purpose, on the other hand, had a standardized coefficient of **0.121**, which was not statistically significant ($p = 0.223$) in the presence of *people*. This suggests that while *purpose* has a positive influence on productivity, its effect was overshadowed by the dominant role of *people* when both variables were considered together.

R-squared

The combined model accounted for 57.5% of the variance in *performance* ($R^2 = 0.575$), indicating that more than half of the variability in productivity can be explained by *people* and *purpose* together.

Solo Predictor Model (Purpose Only)

When *purpose* was tested independently, it became a significant predictor with a coefficient of 0.488 ($p < 0.001$). The solo model explained 27.5% of the variance in *performance* ($R^2 = 0.275$), confirming that *purpose* can independently predict productivity, albeit with less explanatory power compared to the combined model.

These findings positioned *people* as the dominant factor driving productivity, with *purpose* playing a supportive but secondary role.

Second Study Results: Combined Model Only

In the second study, the combined model was sufficient to explain the relationships between the variables, as both *people* and *purpose* emerged as significant predictors. The larger and more representative sample (N = 201) provided greater insight into the dynamics of these predictors.

People

In the second study, *people* retained its strong influence on *performance*, with a standardized coefficient of **0.584**, which was highly significant ($p < 0.001$). This finding reaffirms that factors such as team engagement and social cohesion are critical to driving productivity. The consistency of *people*'s effect across studies underscores its foundational role within the FLOW@WORK framework.

Purpose

Unlike in the pilot study, *purpose* demonstrated a standardized coefficient of **0.304**, which was also highly significant ($p < 0.001$). This indicates that *purpose* played a more prominent role in this larger sample, suggesting that employees' alignment with organizational mission and meaning becomes increasingly relevant in diverse or larger workplace contexts.

R-squared

The combined model explained 66.6% of the variance in *performance* ($R^2 = 0.666$), a notable improvement over the pilot study. This higher explanatory power highlights the robustness of the FLOW@WORK framework when applied to a broader sample.

Key Insights

1. ***People* as the core driver of *performance***: In both studies, *people* consistently emerged as the most influential predictor of *performance*, with strong and significant effects. This underscores the importance of team dynamics, engagement and cohesion in fostering productivity.
2. ***Purpose*'s growing influence in the second study**: While *purpose* had a limited role in the pilot study, its impact increased significantly in the second study. The stronger contribution of *purpose* in the larger sample suggests that alignment with organizational mission may gain prominence in more complex or diverse workplace environments.
3. **Improved explanatory power in the second study**: The combined model in the second study ($R^2 = 0.666$) explained more variance in *performance* compared to the pilot ($R^2 = 0.575$). This improvement reflects the greater precision and representativeness of the second study's findings.
4. **Practical implications:** Organizations seeking to optimize productivity should prioritize cohesive team dynamics (*people*) as a core strategy, while also investing in purpose-driven initiatives to enhance employees' alignment with the organizational mission.

Factor Loadings and Their Interpretation

The confirmatory factor analysis (CFA) conducted on *People, Purpose* and *Performance* confirmed that all three dimensions significantly contribute to the underlying construct of FLOW@WORK. The factor loadings from the pilot and second studies are as follows:

Pilot study results:

- *People*: 0.655 ($p < .001$)
- *Purpose*: 0.456 ($p < .001$)
- *Performance*: 0.546 ($p < .001$)

The pilot study results indicate that *people* had the strongest association with flow, followed by *performance*, and then *purpose*. The high loading for *people* (**0.655**) highlights the critical role of team dynamics, engagement and cohesion in driving flow states. *Performance*, with a loading of **0.546**, plays a moderating role, supporting flow when there is a good match between team skills and task challenges. Finally, *purpose* has a positive but relatively lower loading (**0.456**), suggesting that alignment with the organizational mission contributes to FLOW@WORK, though its impact is more supportive and secondary compared to the other dimensions (see Figure 18.5).

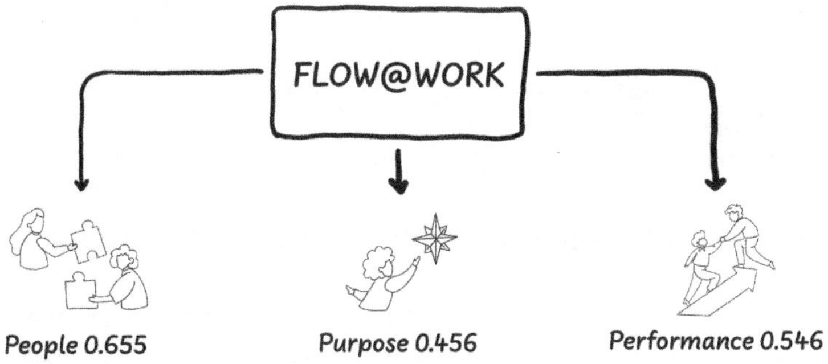

Figure 18.5 Confirmatory Factor Analysis for the 3Ps (Pilot Study)

In the second study, the factor loadings for all three dimensions increased, with *performance* (**0.657**) emerging as the strongest contributor to flow, closely followed by *people* (**0.654**). This marks a shift from the pilot study, where *people* was the dominant driver. Additionally, *purpose* (**0.561**) demonstrated a higher and more substantial contribution compared to the pilot, suggesting that employees' alignment with organizational mission becomes more relevant in larger or more diverse workplace samples. Figure 18.6 demonstrates the loading per factor.

Second study results:

- *People*: 0.654 (p < .001)
- *Purpose*: 0.561 (*p* < .001)
- *Performance*: 0.657 (*p* < .001)

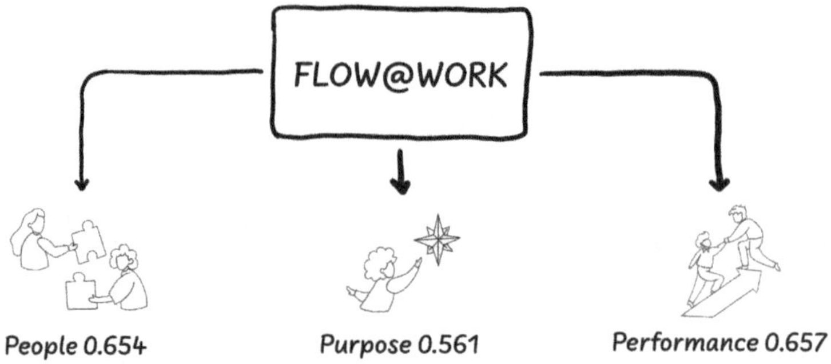

Figure 18.6 Confirmatory Factor Analysis for the 3Ps (Second Study)

Interpretation and Theoretical Implications

People remain a key driver of FLOW@WORK across both studies, emphasizing the importance of team dynamics and employee engagement in creating optimal workplace productivity. However, its contribution is closely matched by *performance* in the second study. *Performance* shows an enhanced role in the second study, possibly reflecting the increased importance of skill-challenge alignment in larger or more varied organizational settings. *Purpose*, while initially less influential in the pilot study, demonstrated a stronger and more consistent contribution in the second study. This highlights the growing relevance of mission alignment as organizations scale or diversify their workforce.

The results from both the pilot and second studies highlight the evolving dynamics of the FLOW@WORK framework. While *people* and *performance* remain central to flow, the increased role of *purpose* in the second study underscores its growing importance in more complex or diverse organizational settings. By leveraging these empirical insights, organizations can better tailor strategies to optimize flow, creating environments where employees are both engaged and productive.

The 3Ps Equilibrium Equation

In addition to the FLOW@WORK formula, which models flow as an interaction of *People, Purpose* and *Performance*, the 3Ps equilibrium equation offers a complementary perspective by treating these dimensions as independent contributors. It captures the cumulative contributions of the 3Ps to team engagement and productivity:

$$\text{3Ps equilibrium} = \textit{People} + \textit{Purpose} + \textit{Performance}$$

Unlike the FLOW@WORK formula, which emphasizes the interaction effects between the dimensions, the 3Ps equilibrium equation assumes that each factor contributes additively to the overall potential for flow.

Rationale for the 3Ps Equilibrium Equation

The 3Ps equilibrium equation provides a simpler yet robust way to evaluate FLOW@WORK. It is rooted in the empirical evidence from both the pilot study and the second study, which highlighted the independent strengths and interrelations of the 3Ps.

Empirical Fit and Unique Insights

The 3Ps equilibrium equation aligns with the following key findings from both studies:

Reliability Analyses

- The high reliability scores (Cronbach's alpha) for all three dimensions across studies confirm their robustness as independent contributors:
  - Pilot: *People* ($\alpha = 0.87$), *Purpose* ($\alpha = 0.88$), *Performance* ($\alpha = 0.82$).
  - Second study: *People* ($\alpha = 0.88$), *Purpose* ($\alpha = 0.88$), *Performance* ($\alpha = 0.87$).

Factor Loadings

- Factor loadings from the CFA further validate the contributions of each dimension:
  - Pilot: *People* (0.655), *Purpose* (0.456), *Performance* (0.546).
  - Second study: *People* (0.654), *Purpose* (0.561), *Performance* (0.657).

These results show that while *purpose*'s contribution increased in the second study, *people* and *performance* remained dominant contributors, reinforcing their cumulative importance.

Practical Applications of the 3Ps Equilibrium Equation

The 3Ps equilibrium equation offers several practical advantages for organizational leaders:

1. **High-level assessments**

   By summing the contributions of *People, Purpose* and *Performance*, this equation provides a straightforward metric for assessing overall workplace dynamics.
2. **Independent diagnosis**

   Leaders can isolate and evaluate gaps in any one of the 3Ps without the complexity of weighted or interaction-based calculations. For example:
   - A low *purpose* score might signal misalignment with the organizational mission.
   - A low *performance* score could highlight skill-challenge mismatches or inefficiencies.
3. **Progress monitoring**

   Organizations can track improvements over time by summing the individual scores of the 3Ps, offering a clear view of changes in team health, alignment and productivity.
4. **Versatility across contexts**

   The simplicity of this model makes it adaptable to diverse organizational settings, from small teams to large, global enterprises. It is particularly useful for environments where leaders seek to understand the independent contributions of the 3Ps without focusing on their interdependencies.

Models and Equations: Weighted and Imbalance Formulas

To complement the FLOW@WORK formula, alternative models explore how different emphases on *People, Purpose* and *Performance* can drive flow in various organizational contexts. These models align with empirical findings from the pilot study (N = 60) and the second study (N = 201), reflecting how organizations might prioritize engagement, alignment or productivity depending on their strategic goals.

1. ***People* imbalance equation: (2 × *People*) + *Purpose* + *Performance***

   This model doubles the weight of *people*, emphasizing the importance of team cohesion, emotional well-being and engagement as primary drivers of FLOW@WORK. It reflects contexts where collaboration, morale and interpersonal dynamics are considered essential to workplace success.

   Empirical alignment

   - **Pilot study:** *People* showed the strongest factor loading (0.655) and the highest correlation with *performance* (r = 0.75) and *purpose* (r = 0.58). These findings validate the centrality of *people* in the FLOW@WORK framework, particularly in smaller or more cohesive teams.

- **Second study:** *People* maintained a high factor loading (0.654) and exhibited even stronger correlations with both *performance* ($r = 0.78$) and *purpose* ($r = 0.70$). This underscores its enduring importance, even as *purpose* and *performance* play increasing roles in larger or more diverse organizational settings.

Strengths: The *people* imbalance equation aligns with organizations that prioritize team cohesion and well-being such as non-profits, creative industries and educational institutions. By amplifying *people*'s role, this model captures the relational and motivational dynamics necessary to foster engagement and collaboration.

Challenges

- Overemphasis on *people* may overshadow the critical roles of *performance* and *purpose*, potentially reducing efficiency or alignment with goals.
- Organizations using this model should monitor productivity metrics to ensure that engagement does not come at the expense of results.

Practical applications

- Ideal for adopting psychological safety, collaboration and employee morale.
- Particularly effective in people-centric industries but must be complemented by productivity-oriented strategies for balanced outcomes.

2. ***Purpose* imbalance equation: *People* + (2 × *Purpose*) + *Performance***

   This model doubles the weight of *purpose*, emphasizing alignment with organizational mission and values.

It resonates with purpose-driven organizations such as NGOs or social enterprises, where mission alignment is prioritized over technical or relational aspects.

Empirical alignment

- **Pilot study:** *Purpose* showed the lowest factor loading (0.456) and weaker correlations with *people* ($r = 0.58$) and *performance* ($r = 0.52$). These findings suggest that *purpose* played a secondary role, making this equation less aligned with the pilot data.
- **Second study:** *Purpose*'s contribution increased significantly (0.561) with stronger correlations ($r = 0.70$) to both *people* and *performance*. These findings support the model's relevance in larger or more diverse organizations but caution against over-emphasis.

Strengths: The *purpose* imbalance equation highlights the motivational and cultural dimensions of flow, making it ideal for organizations where alignment with values and mission is central.

Challenges

- Overweighting *purpose* risks neglecting the relational and technical aspects of flow, potentially leading to inefficiency or a lack of cohesion.

Practical applications

- Use in values-driven organizations or when cultivating a mission-focused culture.
- Combine with strategies that reinforce productivity and collaboration to balance outcomes.

3. ***Performance* imbalance equation: *People* + *Purpose* + (2 × *Performance*)**

Doubling the weight of *performance*, this model emphasizes task alignment, technical expertise and measurable outcomes. It is tailored for organizations were achieving ambitious goals, exceeding benchmarks and maintaining high productivity are paramount.

Empirical alignment

- **Pilot study:** *Performance* had a moderate factor loading (0.546) and a slightly weaker correlation with *purpose* ($r = 0.52$).
- **Second study:** *Performance* emerged as the strongest factor (0.657) and showed significantly higher correlations with both *people* ($r = 0.78$) and *purpose* ($r = 0.70$). These results suggest that as organizations scale or diversify, *performance* becomes more central to driving productivity.

Strengths: The *performance* imbalance equation is well suited for fast-paced, competitive industries such as technology, finance and sales. By amplifying *performance*'s role, it highlights the technical and task-oriented aspects of flow, ensuring alignment with productivity goals.

Challenges

- Over-prioritization of *performance* may lead to burnout, stress or diminished team cohesion.
- Organizations adopting this model must ensure that *people* and *purpose* are not deprioritized, as their absence can reduce long-term sustainability.

Practical applications

- Use in results-driven environments where skill-challenge alignment and outcomes are key.
- Pair with initiatives that promote well-being and engagement to mitigate risks of overemphasis on output.

4. **Balanced FLOW@WORK equation: (1.5 × *People*) + *Purpose* + (1.5 × *Performance*)**

The balanced FLOW@WORK equation offers a middle ground, assigning moderate weights (1.5x) to both *people* and *performance*, reflecting their observed dominance, while maintaining *purpose* as a complementary factor. This equation represents a balanced approach to flow.

Empirical alignment

- **Pilot study:** *People* (**0.655**) and *performance* (**0.546**) were the dominant factors, with *purpose* (**0.456**) playing a secondary role. This suggested that while *purpose* supports flow, *people* and *performance* are the primary drivers.
- **Second study:** Contributions from *people* (**0.654**) and *performance* (**0.657**) became almost equal, while *purpose* (**0.561**) gained prominence, supporting a more proportional distribution. This balanced configuration closely aligns with the empirical findings, making this model highly adaptable.

Strengths: The balanced FLOW@WORK equation integrates team cohesion, productivity and alignment into a unified framework. It is particularly suited for diverse teams or organizations aiming for sustained growth across multiple dimensions.

Challenges

- Few, as this equation avoids overemphasis on any one dimension. However, the nuanced needs of specific organizations may require adjustments.

Practical applications

- Use as a default model in varied workplace settings, particularly those seeking to balance engagement, alignment and performance.
- Effective for organizations that value a holistic approach to team well-being and productivity.

Insights from Model Comparisons

Evolving Contributions Across Studies

In the pilot study, *people* was clearly dominant, while *purpose* played a secondary role. In the second study, contributions were more balanced, with *performance* becoming the strongest factor and *purpose* playing a more substantial role.

Adaptability of Equations

- The ***people* imbalance equation** works well for organizations emphasizing collaboration and well-being.
- The ***purpose* imbalance equation** finds relevance in mission-driven contexts but requires caution to avoid neglecting cohesion and performance.
- The ***performance* imbalance equation** aligns with high-output environments, where measurable outcomes are key.
- The **balanced FLOW@WORK equation** is the most adaptable and supported by both studies.

Practical Utility

Each equation provides tailored insights into how different priorities shape the flow experience. Leaders can choose or combine equations based on their strategic goals, ensuring alignment with team and organizational needs.

Conclusion

The alternative models enhance the utility of the FLOW@WORK framework, providing tailored options to suit diverse organizational contexts. While the balanced FLOW@WORK equation aligns most closely with empirical findings from both studies, each equation offers unique insights into specific priorities. Together, these models allow leaders to optimize FLOW@WORK by aligning their strategies with team and organizational dynamics.

Workplace Pyramid for the Multidimensional *People* Construct

Overview

The multidimensional *people* construct represents a seven-layer model adapted from Maslow's hierarchy of needs, redefined for the workplace. Each layer represents a fundamental category of needs that organizations can address to enhance employee engagement, motivation and satisfaction. The logic behind including the multidimensional people construct was to examine this scale in more detail and uncover how each dimension contributes to the overall *people* concept (see Figure 18.7). The overall scale included 22 items (three to four items per subscale). The facets, definitions and items were as follows:

1. **Security & fairness**
   Definition

   Security and fairness form the foundational layer, focusing on an employee's need for physical and financial security. This includes assurances like a safe working environment, job stability and equitable compensation practices. By meeting these needs, organizations can establish a sense of trust and reduce employee anxiety, allowing them to focus on their roles without fear of unfair treatment or job loss.

   Scale items
   - My organization provides a safe and secure work environment.
   - I am confident in the stability of my employment here.
   - I am happy with my current salary.
   - My compensation is fair and aligns with the responsibilities of my role.

2. **Inclusion & belonging**
   Definition

   Inclusion and belonging address an employee's social needs within the organization, emphasizing acceptance and a sense of community. Meeting this need involves adopting a culture of teamwork and respect, where employees feel valued and integral to the team. A strong sense of belonging enhances engagement and strengthens organizational loyalty.

Scale items

- I feel a strong sense of belonging within my team.
- My organization makes me feel welcome and accepted.
- I feel valued as an individual by my colleagues and supervisors.

3. **Autonomy & control**

Definition

Autonomy and control relate to an employee's desire for independence and self-direction in their work. This need is satisfied when employees have the flexibility to make decisions, manage their own schedules and take ownership of their projects. Granting autonomy empowers employees, boosting motivation and accountability.

Scale items

- I have the flexibility to make decisions in my role.
- I am able to manage my workload in a way that suits me.
- I have ownership over the projects for which I am responsible.

4. **Competence & growth**

Definition

Competence and growth focus on the need for skill development and career progression. Employees in this layer seek opportunities for learning, training and constructive feedback that help them enhance their competencies. Organizations that support growth foster continuous improvement, enabling employees to reach higher levels of expertise and satisfaction in their roles.

Scale items

- My organization provides opportunities for me to develop my skills.
- I receive constructive feedback that helps me improve professionally.
- There are clear pathways for advancement in my role.

5. **Purpose & meaning**
   Definition

   Purpose and meaning reflect employees' desire to align their work and personal values. This is different from the purpose of the overall organization and focuses on a purpose that is personal to each employee. Employees in this layer look for a deeper sense of purpose and want to contribute to a mission they find meaningful. Organizations can fulfil this need by clearly communicating their vision and helping employees understand how their roles contribute to larger, meaningful outcomes.

   Scale items

   - The work I do aligns with my personal values.
   - I feel that my contributions make a meaningful impact.
   - My organization's values align with my values.

6. **Achievement**
   Definition

   Achievement involves the need for goal attainment, recognition and status. Employees in this layer are motivated by reaching objectives and receiving acknowledgement for their accomplishments. By celebrating achievements, organizations reinforce a culture of excellence and performance, satisfying employees' desires for validation and status.

Scale items

- I am recognized for my accomplishments at work.
- My organization celebrates and rewards high performance.
- I feel a sense of accomplishment from reaching my goals.

7. **Self-actualization**
   Definition

   Self-actualization is the pinnacle of workplace needs, where employees strive for personal fulfilment, creativity and realizing their full potential. This layer allows employees to explore innovative ideas, work on passion projects and pursue long-term aspirations. Organizations that encourage self-actualization foster an environment where employees can grow beyond traditional limits, promoting creativity and innovation.

   Scale items

   - My role allows me to explore new ideas and be creative.
   - I am able to work on projects that reflect my personal passions.
   - I feel that I am growing and reaching my potential in this organization.

Figure 18.7 Workplace Hierarchy of Needs: A Multidimensional People Construct

Findings From the Confirmatory Factor Analysis of the Multidimensional *People* Construct

The CFA conducted on the multidimensional *people* construct validated the seven-layer model, demonstrating how each dimension contributes to the overarching concept of *people*. The layers – security & fairness, inclusion & belonging, autonomy & control, competence & growth, purpose & meaning, achievement and self-actualization – showed significant factor loadings, underscoring their importance in fostering workplace engagement, motivation and satisfaction.

The foundational layer, *security & fairness*, had a factor loading of 0.543, indicating its moderate but essential role in building trust and reducing employee anxiety. As the basis of the pyramid, this layer ensures employees feel safe and secure, both physically and financially, creating the stability necessary for engagement and focus. While its contribution is not as dominant as other layers, it is a critical prerequisite for higher-level needs.

Moving upward, *inclusion & belonging* demonstrated a strong factor loading of 0.648. This reflects the importance of raising a culture where employees feel valued, accepted and integral to their teams. Inclusion and belonging fulfil the social aspect of workplace engagement, strengthening team cohesion and organizational loyalty. Organizations that emphasize this layer are likely to experience heightened employee engagement, as individuals thrive in environments that promote acceptance and connection.

Autonomy & control, with a factor loading of 0.494, showed the lowest contribution among the layers. While autonomy is important for workplace satisfaction, this finding suggests it plays more of a supporting role in the *people* construct. Autonomy allows employees to manage their workloads and make decisions independently, but its contribution is secondary compared to relational and developmental dimensions such as belonging or growth. This aligns with research emphasizing autonomy as a factor that enhances engagement rather than driving it outright.

The *competence & growth* dimension emerged as one of the strongest contributors, with a factor loading of 0.741. This highlights the importance employees place on skill development, career progression and constructive feedback. Growth provides a feeling of continuous improvement and mastery, which are key motivators in any workplace. Organizations that prioritize learning opportunities, mentoring and clear career pathways are better positioned to retain talent and enhance employee satisfaction.

The facet of *purpose & meaning* exhibited a factor loading of 0.639, indicating its substantial role in aligning employees' personal values with their work. *Purpose* helps employees find deeper meaning in their contributions, connecting their individual roles to a larger mission. This layer becomes particularly relevant in modern workplaces, where employees increasingly seek meaningful work that resonates with their values. Organizations that clearly communicate their vision and demonstrate how individual efforts contribute to broader outcomes are more likely to inspire commitment and motivation. It is important to note that the 'purpose' facet within the *people*'s construct is simpler and serves a distinct role in this specific model compared to the general independent *purpose* construct.

Achievement, with a factor loading of 0.651, reflected the importance of goal attainment and recognition in driving workplace motivation. Employees derive satisfaction from achieving objectives and receiving acknowledgment for their contributions. By celebrating accomplishments and recognizing high performance, organizations adopt a culture of excellence and inspire continued effort and commitment.

At the pinnacle of the model, *self-actualization* emerged as the strongest contributor, with a factor loading of 0.795. This highlights the transformative potential of workplaces that encourage employees to reach their full potential, explore creative projects and innovate. Self-actualization allows employees to experience fulfilment beyond traditional job roles, driving both personal growth and organizational success. When organizations create environments that enable self-actualization, they unlock unparalleled levels of engagement, creativity and loyalty.

Key Insights and Practical Implications

The results of the CFA reveal a compelling insight into workplace motivation: higher-order needs such as *competence & growth*, *achievement* and self-actualization, which traditionally sit at the top of the workplace pyramid, exhibited the strongest contributions to the *people* construct. Conversely, foundational needs like *security & fairness* and *autonomy & control* demonstrated relatively lower factor loadings, challenging the traditional logic of Maslow's hierarchy of needs. While Maslow's framework posits that foundational needs must be fully satisfied before individuals can focus on higher-order needs, the findings suggest that in workplace contexts, the pursuit of growth, recognition and personal fulfilment holds greater influence over engagement and satisfaction.

Nevertheless, foundational needs remain indispensable as the bedrock upon which higher-order needs can thrive. Dimensions such as *security & fairness* and *inclusion & belonging*, though showing lower factor loadings, play an essential enabling role by fostering stability, trust and inclusivity. Employees must feel secure and valued within their organizations before they can effectively engage with opportunities for development or fulfilment. For example, inadequate compensation or a lack of job security can hinder engagement, even in the presence of opportunities for self-actualization or growth.

The overall findings underscore that in the workplace, higher-order needs often serve as primary drivers of engagement and satisfaction, while foundational needs act as enablers, creating the conditions necessary for higher-order needs to be realized. This shift highlights the unique dynamics of workplace motivation, where employees derive the greatest meaning and motivation from growth-oriented and aspirational opportunities, such as developing new skills, achieving goals and exploring personal potential. Foundational needs, though statistically significant in the CFA, serve as critical prerequisites but do not play as central a role in driving workplace engagement as previously theorized. This insight emphasizes the importance of organizations not only addressing foundational needs but actively investing in initiatives that empower employees to grow, achieve and self-actualize.

Conclusion

The findings challenge traditional assumptions about the sequential nature of needs in the workplace. While foundational needs remain essential, they appear to serve as prerequisites rather than primary drivers of engagement. Instead, higher-order needs like self-actualization, competence & growth and achievement emerge as the most significant contributors to the *people* construct, underscoring their central role in modern workplace motivation.

Organizations should adopt a dual strategy: ensuring foundational needs are met to create stability while actively investing in growth, recognition and fulfilment to inspire and engage employees. By addressing the full spectrum of needs outlined in the workplace pyramid, leaders can create environments that maximize both individual potential and organizational success.

Examining *Purpose* as a Two-factor Scale

An exploratory factor analysis (EFA) on *purpose* revealed that it was plausible to retain two factors to represent the construct of purpose within the FLOW@WORK framework: personal purpose and organizational purpose. These two factors reflect distinct but interconnected dimensions of purpose, highlighting both the intrinsic and collective drivers of engagement and motivation in the workplace (see Table 18.1).

Table 18.1 Two-Factor Exploratory Factor Analysis on Purpose

Item	People purpose	Organizational purpose
I feel that my work contributes to a higher purpose beyond just financial outcomes.	0.942	
I derive a sense of meaning from the impact my work has on others, both within and outside the organization.	0.882	
The work I do aligns with my personal values and what I believe in.	0.692	
I feel that my work supports a purpose that is greater than just day-to-day tasks or immediate goals.	0.650	
The company's mission and values are clearly communicated and guide our work.		0.859
My team's objectives align with the company's purpose, and this clarity drives our collective efforts.		0.840
I clearly understand how my role contributes to the organization's broader goals.		0.672
I am motivated by the purpose and goals of my team.		0.598

Personal purpose represents employees' alignment of their work with their individual values, beliefs and aspirations. Items loading strongly onto this factor highlight the deeply intrinsic motivations employees derive from their roles. For instance, statements such as 'I feel that my work contributes to a higher purpose beyond just financial outcomes' (**0.942**) and 'I derive a sense of meaning from the impact my work has on others, both within and outside the organization' (**0.882**) underscore how meaningful work fosters a sense of personal fulfilment. This factor demonstrates that employees who see their work as aligned with their personal values are more likely to experience motivation and satisfaction.

Organizational purpose, on the other hand, emphasizes alignment with the company's broader mission and shared goals. Items such as 'The company's mission and values are clearly communicated and guide our work' (**0.859**) and 'My team's objectives align with the company's purpose, and this clarity drives our collective efforts' (**0.840**) reflect the importance of clear communication and coherence in organizational vision. The results suggest that employees derive collective purpose and alignment from their team's and organization's goals, reinforcing a shared sense of direction.

These findings confirm that purpose can be explained as a two-factor construct, with personal purpose reflecting the individual, value-driven alignment of employees with their work and organizational purpose representing their connection to the company's mission and objectives. Notably, the *purpose* & meaning facet of the *people* construct aligns closely with personal purpose, as both emphasize the importance of employees finding deeper meaning and value in their roles beyond immediate tasks or outcomes. This overlap underscores the interrelationship between these frameworks and highlights the central role of purpose in workplace engagement. Together, these two dimensions of purpose offer a comprehensive understanding of how purpose operates in the workplace. Organizations that effectively nurture both personal and organizational purpose, alongside related facets like *purpose* & meaning, can cultivate personal fulfilment and collective alignment, driving employee engagement, cohesion and productivity. This dual focus on purpose provides a solid foundation for covering a crucial element of the FLOW@WORK formula.

Understanding the Bigger Picture of FLOW@WORK

The FLOW@WORK framework represents a multidimensional approach to understanding employee engagement, motivation and productivity. At its core, it captures how organizations can utilize flow – defined as a state of deep focus, creativity and satisfaction – by leveraging three interconnected constructs: *People, Purpose* and *Performance.* Each of these dimensions encompasses several critical factors that collectively shape the workplace experience.

In prior analyses, we conducted a CFA to assess the relationships between the 3Ps (*People, Purpose* and *Performance*) and the overarching FLOW@WORK construct. Building on these findings, we revisited the model with key modifications to provide a more comprehensive understanding. The revised model incorporates the multidimensional *people* construct, a two-factor *purpose* construct and *performance* as distinct yet interrelated components. For a detailed breakdown of the results, see Table 18.2.

Table 18.2 Measuring FLOW@WORK: a Deep Dive Into Key Constructs and Metrics

Factor	Estimate	Std. error	z-value	p-value	95% CI lower	95% CI upper
Security fairness	0.541	0.051	10.605	<.001	0.441	0.642
Inclusion belonging	0.631	0.047	13.294	<.001	0.538	0.724
Autonomy control	0.504	0.047	10.823	<.001	0.413	0.596
Competence growth	0.752	0.053	14.207	<.001	0.648	0.856
Purpose meaning	0.649	0.049	13.289	<.001	0.554	0.745
Achievement	0.638	0.047	13.584	<.001	0.546	0.730
Self actualization	0.789	0.055	14.300	<.001	0.681	0.897
Performance	0.632	0.042	14.994	<.001	0.549	0.715
Personal purpose	0.614	0.054	11.275	<.001	0.507	0.721
Organizational purpose	0.590	0.042	13.898	<.001	0.507	0.673

Findings and Closing Thoughts

The findings presented in this table highlight the significant contributions of various constructs to the latent variable FLOW@WORK, emphasizing the multidimensional nature of workplace engagement. Among the constructs, *self-actualization* demonstrated the strongest factor loading (0.789), underscoring its pivotal role in pushing a state of flow by enabling employees to realize their full potential, engage in creative tasks and pursue personal growth. Similarly, *competence & growth* (0.752) was the second highest loading in this model. While foundational constructs such as *security & fairness* (0.541) and *autonomy & control* (0.504) had relatively lower loadings, their significance cannot be overlooked, as they provide the stability and independence required for higher-order needs to flourish. The dimensions of *inclusion & belonging* (0.631) and *achievement* (0.638) further affirm the importance of social connection and recognition in cultivating engagement. Additionally, the purpose-related constructs – personal purpose (0.614) and organizational purpose (0.590) – highlight the dual role of personal alignment and organizational mission in boosting flow. Together, these results validate the comprehensive FLOW@WORK framework, which integrates foundational, developmental and aspirational needs, offering organizations a strategic pathway to enhance workplace engagement and productivity.

Also, while higher-order needs such as self-actualization and competence & growth emerged as the strongest contributors to flow, foundational needs like security & fairness and inclusion & belonging are critical enablers. Organizations must create a stable foundation by ensuring fair compensation, job security and inclusive workplace practices. Once these prerequisites are met, they can focus on providing opportunities for growth, innovation and personal fulfilment. This layered approach ensures that employees can fully engage with aspirational goals without being distracted by unmet foundational needs. Finally, by breaking down the key dimensions – spanning from foundational needs like job security to developmental needs such as skill growth, and finally to aspirational needs like personal fulfilment – the data analysis highlights the nuanced interplay between these elements. This analysis not only validates the multidimensionality of the FLOW@WORK framework but also provides actionable insights for organizations seeking to build environments where employees can thrive and reach their full potential. These findings underscore the importance of addressing both foundational stability and aspirational growth to achieve a workplace culture that consistently drives innovation, satisfaction and productivity.

Part III

Key Takeaways

15 Time for a New Set of KPIs

- **Performance Flourishes in Balance:** True performance arises when people's unique skills align with meaningful purpose and the right level of challenge.
- **Redefine KPIs:** Embrace people-centric KPIs alongside traditional metrics to create a holistic framework that prioritizes employee well-being, growth and impact.
- **Leadership Is a Partnership:** Effective leadership involves co-accountability and co-creation, where both leaders and team members share responsibility for achieving success.
- **Empower Through Recognition:** Celebrating achievements and showing genuine appreciation energize your team, fostering engagement and sustaining high performance.

FlowBite: *When you lead with empathy and purpose, performance follows as a natural by-product of the flow you create.*

16 The FLOW@WORK Equation

- **FLOW@WORK Is Synergy:** Success arises from the harmonious interplay of *People, Purpose* and *Performance*, where each element amplifies the others.

- **Balance Drives Flow:** Optimal flow is achieved when the challenges presented by tasks are matched to the skills and abilities of the team, fostering engagement and peak productivity.
- **People and Purpose Elevate Performance:** Engaged, emotionally connected team members aligned with a compelling organizational purpose are more likely to achieve exceptional results.
- **The Equation for Excellence:** The FLOW@WORK equation – (*People* × *Purpose*) / *Performance* – emphasizes the need for alignment, balance and continuous improvement to unlock organizational potential.

FlowBite: *When* people *and* purpose *align, and* performance *balances challenge with skill, flow becomes not just a state but a culture.*

17 **The 3Ps Equilibrium Equation**

- **Balance Is the Foundation of Success:** Striking equilibrium among *People, Purpose* and *Performance* fosters a thriving and sustainable work environment.
- **Imbalance Has Consequences:** Overemphasizing any one of the 3Ps can lead to disengagement, inefficiency or a toxic culture, emphasizing the need for holistic leadership.
- **FLOW@WORK Is Achieved Through Alignment:** When the 3Ps are in harmony, organizations unlock creativity, productivity and fulfilment, enabling employees and teams to perform at their best.
- **Leadership Is the Art of Equilibrium:** Exceptional leaders guide their teams by supporting individuals, clarifying purpose and maintaining performance standards, ensuring FLOW@WORK thrives.

FlowBite: *True leadership is finding the balance where* people *thrive,* purpose *resonates and* performance *excels – this is the heart of FLOW@WORK.*

18 **Unpacking the Science: Research Foundations of FLOW@WORK and Its Equilibrium Equations**

- **FLOW@WORK Is Built on Balance:** Empirical findings validated the theoretical FLOW@WORK framework of the dynamic interplay of the 3Ps – *People, Purpose* and *Performance* through rigorous statistical analysis; each construct contributes uniquely to the flow experience.
- **People Is Multidimensional:** The multidimensional people construct includes seven distinct layers of workplace needs, highlighting the importance of both personal fulfilment and skill development in workplace dynamics.
- **Higher-Order Needs Take Centre Stage:** Contrary to Maslow's traditional hierarchy, higher-order needs such as self-actualization and competence & growth showed stronger contributions to flow than foundational needs like security & fairness. However, foundational needs remain essential enablers for higher-order fulfilment.
- **Equations to Balance the 3Ps:** The FLOW@WORK equation and the 3Ps equilibrium equation provide actionable frameworks for achieving harmony. These models balance intrinsic motivation, organizational alignment and task challenges, offering tailored strategies for diverse workplace contexts.

FlowBite: *Grounded in science and driven by harmony, FLOW@WORK transforms research insights into informed strategies that empower organizations to thrive.*

Part IV

The Flow Leader

19

Transform the Workplace by Transforming Yourself

Now that you have read about the *flow leadership* philosophy, FLOW@WORK, and the power of the 3Ps, you will have understood that it all starts with *you*. As a flow leader you can raise the awareness of consciousness within your team. By doing so, you have the power to bring out their best potential.

In becoming self-aware you can create an open, communicative environment. Using external awareness allows a greater understanding of how your interactions and communications impact others. Your inner work promotes self-learning and personal growth. In doing so, you are role modelling for your people. In fact, the only way to evolve our workplace is by doing the inner work, to look within to provide the best output. This is what *flow leadership* is at its core.

Great leaders are not born. They do not become effective leaders by reading a book, taking a seminar, or even getting advanced degrees. Of course, education is effective for laying the foundation of business theories and practices. However, there is another journey every flow leader needs to explore. This element is purely internal. *It is the introspective work that needs to be done.*

Elements such as working through cognitive dissonance and building greater empathy can help transform a leader and a workplace. These are some of the soft skills that are easily overlooked. Thankfully, we are seeing new interest from high-level leaders to explore these self-development techniques. At the same time, companies across the globe are looking for better ways to nurture employee engagement and happiness. *Flow leadership* plays a critical role in those improvements.

Throughout your career, have you ever been in a group where someone takes control of the situation by conveying a clear vision and goals? Has this person embodied passion for the work and an ability to make the rest of the group feel energized and performant? Have you noticed how these leaders are not only involved in the process, but they are also focused on helping every member of the group succeed.

Team success is their own success and their main driver. This type of leader garners respect and trust. They inspire the admiration of their teams, superiors, and followers. They help their team develop into the next leader's organization needs and leave in place strong succession plans. They can do so by focusing on and responding to the needs of their team members.

Figure 19.1 Expand Your Vision: Leading with Curiosity and Growth

Equally, flow leaders require intellectual stimulation and personal growth. They love to challenge the status quo and encourage others to think differently. They encourage their teams to explore new ways and learn in the process, getting out of their own comfort zone (Figure 19.1).

Getting back to the idea that you cannot fake true leadership, flow leaders live by their values. And this can be quite the challenge to role model. People are influenced by watching what others do. If they see that your outcomes are achieved, they will attribute this to who you are, what values you hold and the work you put in.

As a result, others will commit to change. They will accept that your strategy works and then mirror those same behaviours. Become that role model, by modelling your own inner work. Inspire change by working on yourself and others will follow. This last section aims at sharing some tips and ideas on how to enhance your *flow leadership* capabilities.

20

Flow Leadership Comes from Self-Awareness

Self-awareness is a beneficial journey for each of us. It can make us better partners, parents and friends. And it can help us lead from a more connected, effective position. Beyond these benefits, however, are the ones experienced by the teams under such leadership. Those teams tend to be successful, happy and loyal.

Flow leaders know how to create a tight link within their teams because they have prioritized their people's well-being. In doing so, they convey both a sense of trust and purpose. These leaders give more to the team and care deeply about the group's ability to accomplish its goals. Turnover tends to be quite low as flow leaders can inspire a great deal of commitment in their followers.

Flow leadership inspires people to achieve the unexpected or reach remarkable results. It gives their teams autonomy over specific responsibilities, as well as the authority to make decisions once they have been trained and coached. This in return induces a positive change in the followers' attitudes and the organization.

As a result, flow leaders will enhance the motivation, engagement, team morale and performance by connecting their team members' sense of identity to a project and to the collective identity of the organization. In return, team members will show support to their leader, emulating their leaders to emotionally identify with them and follow the team norms, without losing any sense of themselves.

As a leader, do not wait for the change to happen. Instead, be the change. Set the trend. Instigate a new beginning if you have not done so already. Action makes change happen, so why not take the first steps towards enhancing your self-awareness?

Figure 20.1 Tuning In: The Power of Self-check-in

Tip 1: 'Self-Check-In' to Become Self-Aware

Self-check-in is a way to give yourself what you give to others (Figure 20.1). It is, in essence, mindfulness for oneself. The more balanced and aligned one is, the more one can give. *Self-check-in* allows for our internal guidance to be heard, our body to be felt, our thoughts and emotions to be acknowledged. In becoming the witness of what is unfolding, we allow for the right actions to be found. And when no more resistance is met, life becomes easier. We enter our *flow*. It is a powerful state of being, one that will always replenish our batteries. Flow is our 'Energizer Bunny'!

Life throws at us many unexpected situations. This is when self-awareness kicks in. It allows us to understand that it is not always the behaviours of others causing our reactions. Rather, when a situation occurs, it is an alarm bell, screaming that there are unresolved parts of us coming to the fore. Entering a zone of *self-check-in* enables us to truly understand our inner narrative, perspective and patterns.

When experiencing a difficult situation, ask yourself:

- *What is the main trigger?*
- *What is really happening?*
- *What is my take on the situation?*
- *What emotions am I experiencing and how am I reacting?*

Tip 2: Identify and Transcend 'Cognitive Dissonance'

In your journey to enhance your self-awareness, working on cognitive dissonance will help you remove any mental frictions. Cognitive dissonance occurs when thoughts and actions are not aligned. Or when beliefs go against actions. Cognitive dissonance is the mental state of being unsettled by conflicting beliefs and actions. Cognitive dissonance results in holding two conflicting ideas, beliefs, values, attitudes or behaviours. As an outcome, it feels as if there is a conflict. It is that uncomfortable tension when holding two opposite thoughts in the brain at the same time. For example, I should spend more time with my kids versus I should spend more time at work.

To better understand this principle, let us look at a few more examples.

If you love eating chocolate but are on a diet, you may feel torn in between wanting to lose weight and indulging. When the mind struggles with such conflicts, we may be experiencing cognitive dissonance.

In the workplace, employees may struggle between often being praised for their excellent contribution and impact in contrast to a persistent feeling of not being recognized both with the adequate title and financial package.

Leaders are not exempt from experiencing cognitive dissonance. It can emerge when an organization's values conflict with personal values. And as the role of a leader is to ensure that their teams implement those company values, a leader can develop cognitive dissonance.

Take another scenario: the aspiration of someone in your team clashes with the reality of a very confined role, restricting chances for career progression. That employee will experience cognitive dissonance as the recognition in between career ambition and the role's current limitation settles in. As a flow leader, you would align professional ambition with the right development plan. In doing so, you would address your employee's purpose and therefore minimize the dissonance.

As a leader over the years, you have most likely worked hard on becoming who you are and developing your leadership style. You may even have read books, invested time, money and energy to better yourself. In return, this boosted your confidence and provided you with the right tools. Imagine that you are now given the challenge to take on a new team. What if that new team was not responding to what you believe is your leadership style? You would find yourself in a challenging situation and may even start to lose patience or become frustrated.

You could start to think that your team is uncooperative, confrontational or resisting the mission and your authority. In that scenario, the issue comes from them; not you. Alternatively, you could take the time to look at the reason why your team is reacting like this and seek out feedback. And in doing so, maybe you would have noticed the cognitive dissonance in between your claims to be a flow leader, putting your people and their well-being first, and your constant and extreme focus on performance disregarding your team's overall well-being. The dissonance occurs in this case between your leadership philosophy and your actual behaviour.

Being open to explore our deeply held beliefs is a crucial leadership skill that any leader should develop now and for the future. As the flow leader that you are, ask yourself where you stand. Challenge yourself and your own limits by finding one deeply held belief and challenge it. When you have found it, become an expert in researching and reading about it. Explore, ask questions, talk about this topic, exchange thoughts and ideas on it. In doing so, you challenge the norm; with such a mindset, you may just find the *next best thing*.

In *flow leadership,* leaders can identify and transcend the issues that cognitive dissonance can create. In an unpredictable world, our minds want to learn things and then rely on those things to always be true. When we are presented with new, conflicting information, this causes stress and reactionary thinking. We may dig into our old set beliefs, rationalizing why we continue to be right. Our minds may look for ways to justify maintaining our long-held beliefs.

Cognitive dissonance is prevalent in the workplace. As you can imagine, it can limit growth and lead us to expend energy on conflicts that do not deserve so much attention. The benefits of recognizing and minimizing the negative effects of cognitive dissonance are great. When we become more socially aware, it provides us with a better understanding on how to crack the cognitive dissonance code. We become better enabled to understand individuals at the core of who they are, what they are made of and what drives them. Then, we can start leading with better knowledge of our teams.

Figure 20.2 Build Your Brain Armour with Mental Immunity

Going against your cognitive dissonance can wear you out and create mental fatigue. Conversely, making mental health a priority can have profoundly positive results on your effectiveness as a flow leader. *Mental immunity* is the state of creating protections (not barriers) that keep the trials of the day from depleting us. The more you can resolve issues before they arise, the more mental immunity you will create (Figure 20.2).

Take a quick quiz to assess if you have cognitive dissonance and, if so, what are they?

Do I have a cognitive dissonance?
What actions would eliminate it?
What part of my behaviour, mindset, beliefs should I work on?
How important is it for me to change my cognitive dissonance?

The more you ask yourself these questions, the more a habit will form in how you think. Introspection is a practice that can become a habit through practice. *Interoception*, the monitoring and understanding of the body's inner workings by the brain, is also a crucial part.

Our brain is continuously monitoring both the external world around us and all the functions, stimuli and needs of the body. Your brain is well equipped to monitor and respond to thoughts. But you can become more in control of your thoughts and how you respond to them.

Tip 3: Openly Share Your 'To Work On' List

To improve your team's cohesion and performance, one way is to inspire others in showcasing how you work on yourself.

Often leaders are afraid to show vulnerability. Instead, they portray themselves as if they were in full control of every aspect of their day to day. I went down that road, and it is exhausting. Not to mention that it is a big fat lie, not only to us but to others. No one is perfect. Rather, let us accept that we are all a work in progress. This screams vulnerability and humanizes the leadership figure.

One of the best tools to encourage your teams to become self-aware is a '*to work on*' list. By sharing the areas that you still need to work on openly, you are encouraging your people to work on their own 'to work on' list. In doing so, you are creating a safe space for your people to be more honest and vulnerable.

A 'to work on' list can gather all topics you have self-identified as areas of improvements, or feedback and advice you have received and are still works in progress. It will take a lot of courage to openly sharing openly some of the feedback and tips received. Strangely, it also makes it more bearable (Figure 20.3).

Figure 20.3 Show and Grow: The Power of the 'To Work On' List.

Each point added to your list should be met with a solution and an indicator of success to help you identify if it has been addressed or not. We do so because there is nothing more satisfactory than crossing out an item on a 'to work on' list. It means that you have succeeded at transcending a work in progress point and achieved growth.

On my list, my first topic was to become more strategic and less operational. At the time, when I received that feedback from my CEO, my ego was crushed. It hurt because I took pride in thinking that I was strategic. And while I may have been, what I did not do was to cater my message to the target audience. It often resulted in sharing too many operational details to a senior leadership audience. Such feedback is valuable. It helps you recalibrate and, with time, integrate a new way of thinking and working.

Other feedback that I received over the years was to slow down and pace myself. Often, I was going too fast and not checking in with my team. As a result, I would lose people along the way and create inefficiencies. Once I was made aware of this by my team, during each meeting, I would then stop many times, smile and ask them if I was going too fast. They would smile and take this opportunity to then ask more questions and rephrase what had been discussed.

To help me slow down even more, together we introduced the notion of the *red card*. Whenever I was going too fast and losing people, they could pull out their *red card* and call me out. It worked; it forced me to always become present and self-aware. It equally empowered my team to call me out anytime.

To channel my ideas is another feedback that I received over the years. Being an agent of change means that my passion lies in challenging norms and disrupting for the greater good. With this ability comes the downside to having a very active and creative mind. Each new idea could become a new project. And each new project added to the list generated more work. And yet great for the system, it was exhausting for my team.

To protect them from my creative mind, I started to put down any new ideas on a notepad. I would then look at the overall project list and decide if my new ideas were worth sharing and pursuing. Sometimes it was not. Sometimes it was, but the moment was not the right one, so I would park it. In doing so, I was forcing myself to become self-aware and aware of my team's needs.

Whatever the solution is, you will need to create a new habit. Change will not come easy, but when it does, it is a small victory. And in the process, do not get scared of asking for feedback. Whatever the feedback is, receive it and act on it. It is an opportunity for growth. Share your status and progress of your 'to work on' list. Ask your team to help you stay on the right path. In giving them permission to call you out, they will help you become self-aware at times you thought you were but, in fact, were not.

Take a moment to start your own 'to work on' list:

What is on your self-identified areas of improvement?
What advice/feedback have you received that you can add to your 'to work on' list?
. . .

Tip 4: Recondition Your Beliefs

Emotional intelligence (EQ) is essential in *flow leadership*. With greater social awareness, the leadership world is being reshaped. Flow leaders possess what is referred to as the social brain, which includes a perspective that leads to higher connectivity and helps fuel more social awareness and empathy. And empathy is one of the components of what is broadly termed EQ, together with self-awareness, motivation, self-regulation and social skills.

Self-awareness is that deep knowing and understanding of your own feelings and acceptance that your emotions are part of your human experience. When leaders are aware of their own feelings, they can better acknowledge and pick up on the feelings of their team members and what the root causes of any problematic feelings might be.

If self-awareness is about understanding and acceptance, self-regulation is the ability to manage emotions. If your own emotions cannot be tempered, how can you handle the ones of your team members or your clients?

In addition, flow leaders have strong social skills. The ability to decipher feelings, without the ability to communicate them will not enable you to resolve the disagreement or misunderstanding at hand.

Emotional intelligence is the ability to recognize and understand our own emotions and the emotions of others. It helps us discern between different feelings and to use this emotional information to guide our thinking and adjust emotions to achieve goals. By being in tune with such EQ, a leader can be more aware of the needs of those around, team members and clients alike.

Emotional intelligence is what brings out the best in others and pushes leaders to become even more inclined to adapt to neurodiversity and changes in the world around us. That means that those leaders are not only more in touch with themselves, but they are also especially more in touch with the needs, emotions and intentions of others around them. If you have worked in a corporate office environment, you probably already know why effectively reading people's emotions and exhibiting empathy can be helpful.

Leaders with high EQ are far more socially tuned in and therefore have a better grasp on individuals around them and who they are. They are better prepared to lead with greater insight into the emotions and motives of their teams. They have become much more specialized in their approach to cognitive problem-solving and conflict resolution regarding the daily challenges in the workplace.

These new superpowers are a crucial asset for a leader. The social brain calls for the neurons in the brain to be closer and to fire together in concise harmony. These neural connections have been reorganized to disregard irrelevant synapses and preserve and enhance the important ones.

This helps leaders become better at processing critical information and operate in the corporate world reliably and more effectively than ever before.

Emotional intelligence is essential to effective leadership. There are managers in business who, although driven to meet the goals of the company financially, lack the emotional cognitive powers to be empathetic towards their people. They lack the social awareness to be a leader that can gently lead their team to walk where they walk, rather than where they point.

On the other hand, there are leaders who demonstrate and practice EQ in the workplace. Two come to mind: Indra Nooyi, CEO of PepsiCo, for her gratitude towards her people and their parents, and Satya Nadella, CEO of Microsoft, for his empathy and way of turning mistakes into learnings. Those leaders can create a sense of community, belonging and *oneness*. Having the strongest business acumen yet failing at EQ will not result in the optimal output your organization needs. We are just beginning to understand the many ways EQ plays a role in effective leadership. But we do know it makes for more productive communication, less stressful environments, and more self-awareness and maturity.

21

Who You Are Is How You Lead

Emotional intelligence and conscious leadership, coupled with the knowing of who you are, are essential. Who you are is how you lead. This creates self-awareness and the emergence of self-management.

Business performance improves when leaders can decipher emotions and respond to different problems using different styles. Those leaders are the kind who did the work themselves first. By growing first as a person, a leader can inspire change and lead by example, paving the way ahead. Working on oneself is only one part of the equation. The other part is about witnessing and understanding our impact on others.

Tip 1: From Self-Awareness to External Awareness – Understand Your Impact on Others

Words, actions and tone of voice can have a tremendous impact on others. Emotions are contagious and often create a chain reaction. External awareness is recognizing that your behaviour affects your people. To witness and understand this reality, you will need to pause and look at the reactions of others during meetings and discussions. Forget about what they answer or say; instead, pay attention to their facial expressions and body language which can indicate how they are feeling.

Proceed with *active listening*. Look at what is not being said. What is their body language telling you? Decipher the invisible by tuning in truly and genuinely to what your people are experiencing simply because you care. Have the others' interests at heart and do not interpret what is happening through the filter of your own emotions. In the beginning, ask for feedback and questions to validate your assumption. Over time, you will be able to read the room more accurately as you progress with the work on yourself.

Seeking feedback is a first step towards establishing a healthy and transparent discussion. Asking for feedback is tough, scary and very uncomfortable. Yet feedback is paramount to understand how you impact others. This bold move will allow you to evolve as a leader. Most importantly, it will bring you closer to your team. And we must not forget that it is also the most straightforward path to personal growth.

It can often be daunting to ask others for feedback on yourself, particularly when it is your work team. But once you do the internal work, you will be much more prepared to use their feedback and see it as constructive criticism. It is also good to keep in mind that none of us is perfect. If you are willing to do the work and are open to improvement with your team, they will see that. And this is a key part of the process. Every time I asked my teams to give me feedback, I tried to show them that I was willing to evolve for the greater good of the team.

Asking for input can begin with asking your team to fill out a questionnaire on their experiences as employees. This can evolve into roundtable discussions and greater exploration.

Do not worry if everyone seems intimidated to start! I know first-hand how awkward this process can be in the beginning, but once you gain the trust of your team, the energy will quickly switch to one of enthusiasm and excitement.

In all my roles, what I cared for the most was my people and how I could serve them better as a leader. To achieve this objective, I often stood up in front of my teams to seek their live feedback. I would give them a flip chart, leave the room and ask them to openly share their feedback. A scary experience for sure, but what a way to grow and learn how to put the ego on the side. This exercise however will not work unless trust has been built.

In my mind, this process was only fair. If my teams and people are put each year under performance review, why should they not be given the chance to share their feedback? While it is the case in some companies, it is truly not the norm today. Or when it is implemented, it is out of an HR measure due to a potential situation or concern with a manager. What if feedback tools could be rolled out as a small part of the journey to becoming a flow leader?

That process would allow for the leader to be coached on how to receive feedback to better understand its value and change their perception of feedback as a negative experience that highlights what they have not done. Instead, we can begin to see it to continue growing as a better leader and as a better human being.

Take a moment to ask yourself:

When was the last time that you asked for feedback?
Have you ever asked your HR department to run a 360-degree evaluation of you as a leader?
How did you react to that feedback?
What did you do with it?

The richness of receiving feedback is clearly undervalued and should be fully integrated in any organization. For this same reason one of my favourite workshop tools is *The Moment of Truth*. It is a three-minute speed meeting, during which all team members, including the leaders, must sit in pairs and take turns providing advice.

The objective is to share with one another what one values in the other and as a second step, share what the other could adjust or opportunities for growth. While feedback looks at the past, advice tends to focus on the future and helps us shape it.

This exercise may sound a bit untraditional, but in my experience, it is extremely beneficial and powerful. It creates a stronger bond between intra-team members, shows that truth can be told, and allows any latent issues to come to the surface and be fixed.

During that exercise, as a leader, you will need to encourage each of your team members to provide *you* with comments. During the first few seconds, you will witness hesitation. When this happens, gently nudge them. You can even volunteer starting points that you know they could provide you advice on. Reassure them that it is okay and safe to share. With each bit of information received, accept it and use it. Relay it during your next meeting, making it something to smile about. This technique will allow you to guarantee transparent feedback next time around!

At the end of the exercise, think of compiling all feedback received and asking your team for their help. This could be added to your '*to work on*' list. To receive feedback and not act on it creates the status quo. Rather, set your heart on transforming this feedback into growth opportunities.

If you seek feedback, be ready to deal with it, or else do not ask. If you give feedback, do not hesitate; share it raw, no need to sugar-coat everything. But do it respectfully. Some feedback will be more difficult to address and put a specific action behind. It will make you realize that sometimes you think you do well and try your hardest, yet you still manage to fall short on expectations.

That feedback is in fact the most valuable. It shakes you to the core and makes you question how you could have done better. Once, I was simply told by one of my team members who had just resigned: 'I respect you, but we never clicked. We never found a way to work together, a way to communicate, a way to settle.' It was tough to hear. I felt very saddened and upset; moreover, as I did not share that perspective.

However, she had the courage to stand her ground, express herself and share what was in her heart. This is worth celebrating and a testament to the dialogue loop created. As a leader, I am sure that I could have done better. I am sure that somehow along the way I must have let her down. At that time, all I could think of was the following sentence: 'People do not quit jobs, they quit people.' She had quit me and my inability to give her what she was seeking, dreaming of and expecting from her job.

Figure 21.1 Feedback: The Handshake that Fuels Growth

Reality is that when a company embraces feedback as part of its culture, misunderstandings are minimized. Feedback is easier to give and receive if there is a strong underlying relationship and trust between people. This is another great reason to invest time in developing such relationships (Figure 21.1).

Receiving feedback is a skill you can develop. We should be able to take feedback and learn from it. Regardless of how it is delivered, we should be able to listen, accept the lesson, distance it from our ego and move on. Instead, we often listen, pretend we are fine and then brew on it for hours. Why? Simply because it hurts our *ego*. If, however, we were to accept that every interaction, positive and negative, is a source of growth, our ego would vanish, and so would the pain associated with this process. It is, as we have seen many times throughout this book, a matter of perspective.

Tip 2: *People* Before Paperwork and Process

Empathy is not just for HR professionals! Empathy is a critical skill, considered a soft one that every leader needs to have. Empathy has now become a core competency expected of all business leaders. In fact, leaders who practise the art of empathy are the next generation of flow leaders. They are essential for a company's growth strategy and for the well-being of employees. Empathetic leaders not only have more visionary and productive teams, but they are also most likely to build loyalty among their best employees.

They will connect with the feelings of others even if they may not be able to resolve the problem at hand; they would have tried hard. Empathy is therefore a true enabler and enhancer of employee and work engagement and your customer experience. Showcasing such a value will inspire others to do the same internally and externally.

The gift of empathy is not how you relate to the experience or the person. It is how you connect to the emotions – the feelings that crystallize what the other person is experiencing. Empathy is not the same as sympathy, which can be seen as feeling sorry for someone else. Instead, it is about connecting at an emotional level (Figure 21.2).

Figure 21.2 Soul to Soul: The True Power of Empathy

To show empathy does not mean that you must agree with the content or what you are asked to do. You can even disagree and stick to your boundaries. Saying no is completely acceptable and does not prevent you from displaying empathy. As a leader, in some instances, there will be a business need to take actions you know your clients or employees may dislike. Under such circumstances, the tone you take will create the difference. When you remain compassionate and keep a humane perspective, your message will be more smoothly received.

Empathy is a dance between people. Beyond the content, the tone and the functional aspect of the interaction, it is mainly about the meaning and value both sides place on it. It is accepted that there are three different types of empathy: cognitive, emotional and compassionate. Regardless of which type, the end game is to take the most compassionate action you can, reflecting your customers' and people's needs. This is how rapport and trust are established.

To inject empathy throughout organizations, there is no miracle one-size-fits-all approach. If we believe emotions are contagious (especially when transmitted from top management), then its success relies heavily on leadership from the very top. And this is where the challenge lies!

However, if the top management embraces the importance of empathy, they will see this quality spread throughout the organization. My corporate experience shows employees with strong empathy skills are also more productive and innovative. So, if your objective is to increase efficiency and expand the number of solutions that you can solve for your customers or employees, you want to hire employees with this and other strong *soft skills* such as active listening, emotional intelligence or problem-solving, for example.

Empathetic companies will experience better retention and higher morale among employees. This is rather essential in the context of today's market reality. The quest to find the right talent is difficult. Today's workforce is asking for empathy as a prerequisite for their satisfaction and commitment to the company. Similarly, Gen Z employees are more likely to stay with an empathetic employer. And they are our future at work, are they not?

To really make a change, the first step is to want to understand where others are coming from, to gain their perspective. When you focus on wanting to understand your colleagues or your customers, you can cultivate empathy in your own sphere of influence. This can have a big impact on your team and brand.

If a team systematically fails to display empathy towards their internal and external customers, maybe the best approach is to ask oneself what is preventing them from being empathetic. What are the roadblocks on their path to empathy.

Often, by asking the right questions, as seen in Part I, barriers and obstacles will come to light. Only by knowing what is at hand can teams then find the relevant solutions together. If two people look at the same problem using different filters, they will not see the situation in the same way. This is why changing your own perspective can have a dramatic and positive impact; it can be a step towards enabling everyone to show empathy.

The introduction of Teams and Zoom video calls during the pandemic had its benefits. It humanized the fact that beyond an employee is a real person, with a full life and unique needs. Discovering the lives of the employees outside of work broke barriers. We realized that we all share the same human experience. This is a key part of being empathetic. This is the perfect opportunity to connect beyond work and to become curious enough to form a bond.

In doing so, you will notice how you, as a leader, can make a difference in your people's lives. Accommodating other people's needs before they ask you to is an effective way to acknowledge the human factor and acknowledge the importance of your team members. In fact, when we nurture connection, we cultivate wisdom over knowledge, thus leading to discovery and compassion.

Heavy workloads, long hours, job insecurity and emotional change are the perfect ingredients for disaster. This is exacerbated when people start lashing out at one another, creating a ripple effect and a toxic environment. As a leader it is important to know when and how to inject positivity and happiness to alleviate the exhaustion and suffering your team may be experiencing.

To find the best remedy, start by paying attention to what is said, what is written and the tone of emails – ensure that there is no room for interpretation. Do not cut off any team members when they speak and give room for everyone to express themselves. Maybe instead of starting your next project review with the most senior team member, ask your most junior team member to talk about their projects first. Make them shine and understand how valued they are. There are many ways to display inclusivity.

A simple change like this changes the norm and initiates a healthier team dynamic. Everyone is given time and space to be. Remember, emotions are contagious. Spread empathy. Lead by example. Be the change. Awareness of each of your team members' situation will help you better assess their needs.

This is what will ensure that your people are not only aware of what is happening but feel included. They need to relate and feel part of the system. Create a signature approach based on your own team's dynamics. Be creative and challenge the norm. In designing the unexpected and investing in your team in this way, you will keep your team's energy level up, everyone's commitment high.

This is how you create and maintain FLOW@WORK. Listen to your people and ask questions. Taking those extra minutes in meetings to build camaraderie – hear your team members out, provide comfort, share advice and talk nonsense or laugh. This is what will build a stronger and more resilient team that can withstand challenges and a culture that inspires better business.

22

Earn Your *People*'s Trust

Focusing on internal work and your impact on others are key components to becoming a flow leader, but one must also build trust. Model the behaviour you expect from your team. Allow your team to understand your vision with clear speech, uncluttered by jargon and based on scenarios your team can relate to and connect with. The clearer your articulation, the better chance you have of winning them over and the foundation for building trust.

Getting your team buy-in is always the first step for any leader.

Tip 1: Stand Up for Your Team

In my two decades of ascending the corporate hierarchy, I have often felt frustrated by the lack of courage in some leaders. As senior leaders, we are compensated for our strategic acumen and business expertise. Alongside these privileges comes an equal responsibility to strongly support our team members.

Far too often, I have found myself in what I call *painful meetings*, witnessing the unwarranted scrutiny and criticism of more junior team members by senior leadership. Should not senior leaders step in when their team members face unfair challenges or criticism from higher-ups?

Leadership demands more than just supervision; it necessitates active advocacy and solidarity. Showing a united front in support of team members is not just fair; it is the most expedient path to building trust and fostering a cohesive team environment.

The most effective leaders are those who hold themselves accountable. Taking ownership of challenges and standing up for team members not only demonstrates leadership prowess but also significantly strengthens team trust and morale. This proactive approach to leadership not only ensures organizational success but also cultivates a culture of mutual respect and collaboration.

This topic hits home for me because I have experienced first-hand the impact of leaders who lack courage or fail to stand up for their team members. One incident stands out vividly in my mind, a situation that shaped my perspective on leadership forever.

Early in my career, I was part of a project team tasked with a critical client deliverable. Our team had put in long hours, worked through weekends and poured our collective energy into crafting a solution we believed in, reviewed and approved by our team leader. However, during the final presentation to senior management, things took an unexpected turn.

One of our team members, a talented and hardworking individual, was grilled relentlessly by a senior executive. The questions were not just probing but bordered on hostile, highlighting every minor flaw in our work. It was as if all our efforts were being torn apart in front of us. What struck me most was the silence of our own team leader, who sat through the meeting without uttering a word in our defence.

After the meeting, the team was deflated, questioning our abilities and the value of our hard work. It was a turning point for me. I realized then that being a leader is not just about having strategic acumen or business skills; it is about having the courage to stand up for your team, especially in difficult situations.

Fast forward to my role as a senior leader, I made a conscious decision to never let my team face such situations alone. I remember a time when a junior team member was being unfairly criticized during a project review. Instead of staying silent, I stepped in, acknowledging our collective effort and addressing the concerns raised with a balanced perspective. It was not about shifting blame but about fostering a culture of support and accountability (Figure 22.1).

Figure 22.1 Weathering the Storm: Leading with Shelter and Support

Writing about this experience, I reflect on the importance of leaders showing up for their teams. It is not enough to just delegate tasks, mentor and expect results; true leadership means standing by your team, advocating for them and building trust through actions, not just words.

Through my journey climbing the corporate ladder, I have learnt that the most effective leaders are those who are not afraid to hold themselves accountable, who understand that their success is intertwined with the success of their team. It is a lesson I carry with me every day and one that I hope resonates with leaders at all levels.

Tip 2: Create Co-Responsibility and Co-Accountability

Co-responsibility and co-accountability are vital to your company's success. In co-sharing responsibility and accountability, leaders and employees jointly must reach the company's objectives. It becomes a collective endeavour, removes leadership fatigue and increases employee empowerment and recognition.

When employees are held accountable for doing what they are supposed to do, it breeds trust among individuals and teams. *People* can start counting on each other, whether that means meeting deadlines, fulfilling duties or feeling comfortable enough to approach a co-worker or manager for help. Asking for help is an enormous win. It means that the space you have created is safe enough.

When everyone from the top to the bottom follows through on promises, does not blame others for mistakes and supports others in achieving goals, it creates a healthy and positive work culture. As a result, this generates trust and enhances productivity.

And when members of an organization are held accountable and responsible for their own actions, it promotes a positive team culture. Additionally, it establishes the foundation for a healthier, happier and safer working environment. *People* can focus on their work instead of having to deal with colleagues' inappropriate actions or behaviours.

Co-accountability and co-responsibility can help improve your bottom line. When time is not wasted on identifying the sources of problems or waiting for someone to decide, every single individual can devote more energy to their own respective projects, pushing the company's business forward.

In co-sharing responsibility and accountability, a very strong message is spread. It becomes a source of inspiration and motivation for everyone to exceed their goals and performances. They know that they cannot rest on their laurels. Because they have been empowered, they feel responsible and accountable. Moreover, they feel ownership towards the business and want to outdo the company's competition.

Co-accountability can be embedded by making everyone in the team feel responsible. It enables the leader to establish meaningful goals and set clear expectations. For many employees, it is easier to hide behind excuses. When team members are not empowered, the responsibility lies solely with the leader. This can be draining for the leader and energy-depleting for the team members who act and behave as true subordinates. By injecting this notion of co-responsibility and co-accountability, you will break the cycle of codependency and maximize your team's efficiency.

Prior to starting the journey of building co-accountability and co-responsibility, the first step though is to define what it means for your business and within your team. One way to do so is to establish a set of *team rules* which will need to be signed and followed by each team member. What could go wrong if my people are not held accountable? Where would my team need leeway to be innovative and creative? From there, you should agree to set clear goals, expectations and guidelines for everyone to follow.

The rules should be clearly articulated and consequences listed if they are not followed. While for some team members the notion of being co-responsible and co-accountable may be already integrated or come easily, expect that for others the learning curve may be longer.

It can be a daunting task, especially if any team members are disengaged. It is, however, of crucial importance to make certain they become on par with the others (Figure 22.2).

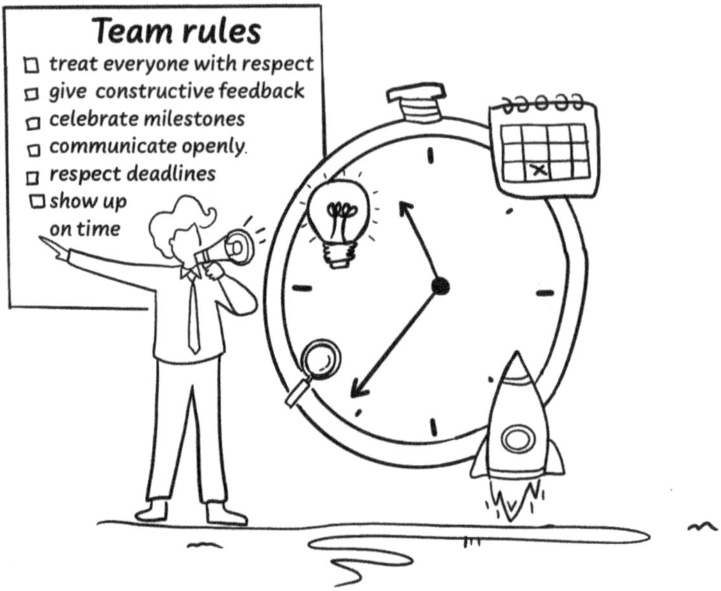

Figure 22.2 Broadcasting the Blueprint: Announcing Team Rules for Collective Success

For starters, co-accountability and co-responsibility promote ownership. Employees know their responsibilities and understand the expectations. Ownership teaches them the value of their work and ensures they start taking pride in it. What I noticed is that often the more junior team members do the work, and the more senior ones get the credit. Is that motivating for the junior members? If they were to do the work, and as a leader you explain how their work fits into the bigger picture, put them forward to present if possible, or if not, add their name to the work.

What do you think would happen if you did this? It shows that you trust them enough to let them shine.

When the framework is clear, the team knows exactly what to do daily, so it eliminates time wasted on deciding what to work on and in what order. Throughout the process and after, your team will become more engaged, motivated and productive, churning out higher-quality work.

Being a high performer, constantly in search of excellence, I have a hard time accepting poorer quality of work. While this may put pressure on some, it also establishes the standards. In setting clear expectations, people are confronted with standards and adopt them for themselves. There is little need for outside interference. Your people will aim to make themselves and you proud of their work and behaviour.

23

From Theoretical Values to a Behavioural Set of Principles

Values are fundamental principles that guide behaviour, choices and interactions within an organization. They shape the culture and identity of a company. They encompass business beliefs, principles and decisions. Values shape the perceptions of employees, potential hires, customers, stakeholders and business partners. As a leader, it is paramount to work with values and recognize that brand values can evolve over time, especially during organizational transitions.

Rather than being static statements in a brand book or on an intranet, values should be dynamic. They offer behavioural guidelines and an actionable philosophy, directing how individuals and teams should act and make decisions in the day-to-day operations of the organization. The importance of values lies in their capacity to guide decision-making, shape culture, define identity, build trust and drive accountability. In essence, values are not just words on paper. They are the living and breathing DNA of your organization, influencing how individuals and teams behave as they collectively work towards shared goals.

Tip 1: Navigate the World of Values

Oftentimes, recalling company values can be difficult. And even if remembered, putting them into action might be a challenge. The primary reason for this is that, unfortunately, they often stay at a theoretical stage. Therefore, prior to assessing their practical application, let us focus on basic awareness and do an exercise in self-assessing how well you know your company values (Figure 23.1).

Can you list your company values off the top of your head?
Do you understand their meaning and significance?

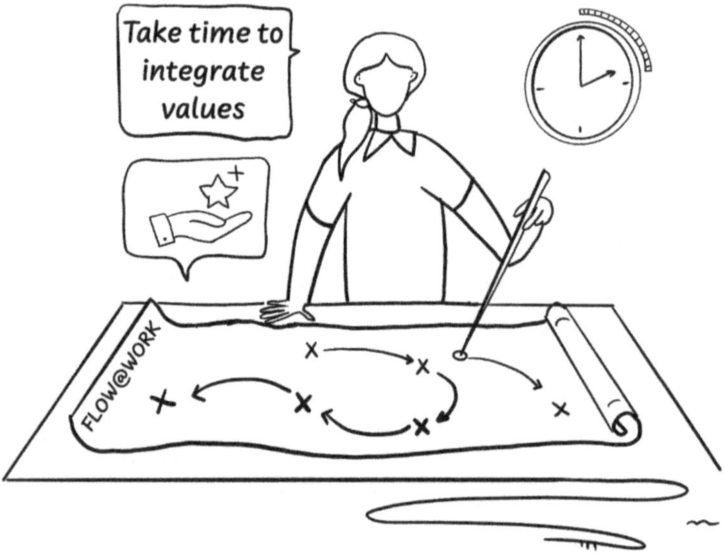

Figure 23.1 Exploring the Map: Integrating the World of Values

Let us continue.

- *If your values are aligned with the ones of the company, ask yourself: how do your personal values complement the company's mission and objectives?*
- *Do your aligned values enhance your job satisfaction and performance?*
- *If your values are misaligned with the ones of the company, where do you perceive the misalignment between your values and those of the company?*

- *Has this misalignment impacted your daily work, and if so, how and to what extent?*
- *Are there specific aspects of your role or the company culture that clash with your values?*

These scenarios and questions aim to prompt reflection on the alignment of personal values with those of the company, providing insights into the impact on individual well-being and job satisfaction. Leaders who take the time to integrate values into their work reality will foster a values-driven culture within the organization.

Tip 2: Examine How Your Values Have Permeated the Organization

Values in *flow leadership* and under the FLOW@WORK framework are looked at an individual, team and organizational levels. And the closer the alignment, the less resistance there will be. This increases the likelihood of turning theoretical values into behavioural ones (Figure 23.2).

As a first step, it is critical to take a moment to reflect.

- *Can you provide specific examples of how you integrate these values into your daily leadership practices?*
- *How do your actions, guided by these values, influence your team's dynamics and performance?*
- *Are your team values explicitly defined?*
- *Do they align with the overall organization's values and the values of the individuals in your team?*

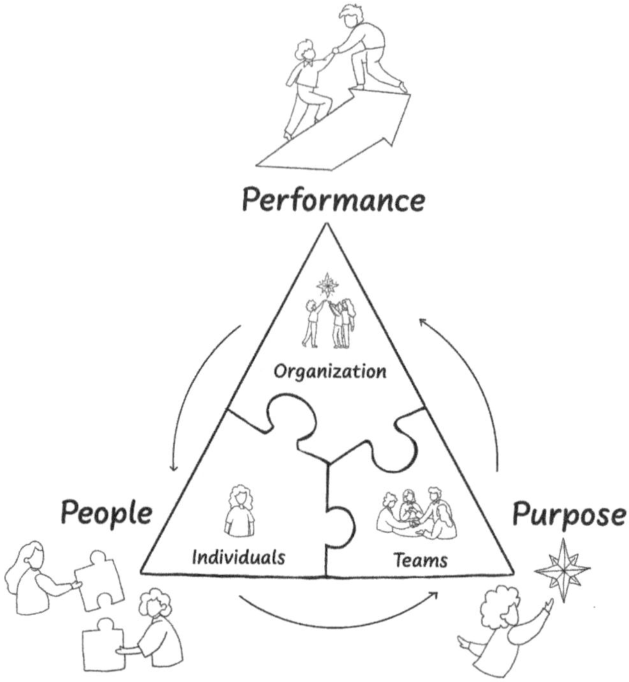

Figure 23.2 Connecting the 3Ps – *People, Purpose* and *Performance*: The Triangle of *Flow Leadership* in Organizations

When assessing the clarity and alignment of values, proceed with one layer at the time.

Start with the first layer which is the foundation of the overall organization. Your *people*.

- *Are your people aware of the company's values?*
- *Do they understand the meaning and what to make of those values?*
- *Do they know what the values stand for?*
- *And are they aware of their own values?*
- *Do their personal values align with the ones of the team and overarching organization?*
- *Can individuals provide examples of how they integrate those values at work?*

- *Are they referring to those values when making decisions or during interactions?*

Then move up to the second layer, which represents your teams.

- *Do your team members collectively understand the company values?*
- *Are they clear on your team values?*
- *Are team behaviours consistent with team and company values?*
- *How are team values communicated and reinforced?*
- *Do team members refer to values for problem-solving or when collaborating?*
- *Are teams recognized or rewarded for embodying those values?*

Your last layer is the third one, which is your overarching company.

- *How well are those values integrated into the overall organizational culture?*
- *Are values consistently applied across different departments and teams?*
- *Do leaders actively promote and embody those values?*
- *Have your values evolved or been adapted over time to meet any new organizational needs or business transformations?*
- *Do you measure and monitor how those values affect your organization's performance and overall employee satisfaction?*

Asking these questions at various levels helps gauge the depth of understanding, alignment and practical application of values throughout the organization. It provides insights into the effectiveness of the values in shaping behaviours and decision-making.

Tip 3: Raise the Awareness on Your Company Values

If your company values are not known, then the top priority should be about increasing their awareness. To display and market them could be a first step. Create a story. Make them exciting and visible in your workplace. Instil your values through the hiring and onboarding process. It portrays not only what your company stands for, but it equally helps you select the right people who will naturally align with your brand values (Figure 23.3).

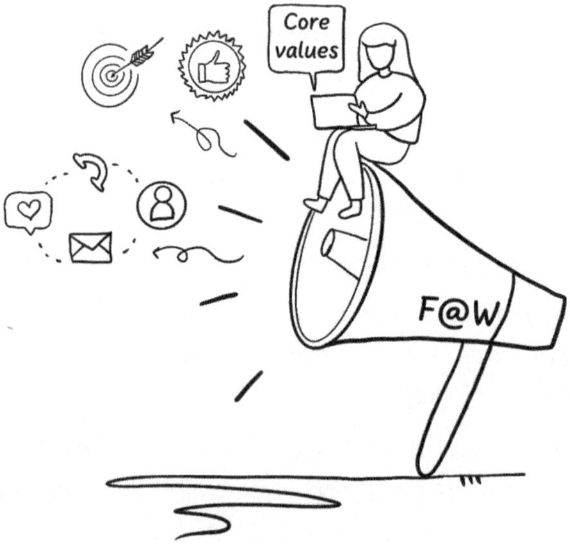

Figure 23.3 Amplifying the Message: Broadcasting Core Values Loud and Clear

How you communicate your brand values is as important as establishing what they are. Communicating them effectively is a hurdle that is important to overcome. To sum up, a company should ensure that its core values are part of any communication strategy. If this cumbersome process is not done, all the work done in defining those values will not pay off.

Tip 4: From Brand Values to Service Philosophy

If the challenge is that your company values are known but not acted upon, translate them into behavioural guiding principles. To facilitate engagement, turn your company values into simple and actionable behavioural principles. Use the company values to measure and drive performance. Turn them into a simple and powerful set of measures that allow for everyone to be accountable. To do so, take your company values and translate them into a service philosophy.

A *service philosophy* is how every employee can live and breathe your company values. It is about how every employee in any company plays a part. A service philosophy is a framework used to translate brand values into the job and how those are implemented. It will guide any employees to know how one should speak, behave, react, write, serve, etc. It is, in essence, a set of guiding principles that an organization uses to solve support issues, build customer relationships and mitigate relationships.

It is a bit like a beacon that directs your every single interaction with your internal and external clients. It is the most direct and powerful way to empower any of your employees to feel confident when facing partners or clients. It blurs the line between the front and back office to create a seamless experience for anyone in your company (Figure 23.4).

Figure 23.4 Building Blocks of Service: Assembling Your Philosophy Brick by Brick

While there are many ways to implement a service philosophy, I have found that the most efficient way is to host workshops, virtual or in person, across all departments and markets on a company-wide level. A key component for success is to integrate role plays and practise them during your workshops. It will guarantee that your values are integrated into your employees' daily routines and enable your team members to better understand what those values mean for them and their jobs.

From abstract, theoretical values, individuals and teams can understand how they relate to them and what to make of them. A key milestone for attendees is to co-create their department's application of your overarching company service philosophy. Such a process inspires change and ensures that your teams will embrace, live and act by those values. This process will empower your employees to adhere to the behavioural values of your company.

In addition, they will start making meaning of those values from a *service* point of view. Service does not only apply here to external partners or clients, but it also relates to the inter-departmental collaboration. It will reinforce the principle of co-accountability and co-responsibility to work by those values.

Tip 5: Practise What You Preach!

In *flow leadership*, being real and true to yourself is essential. A flow leader should show these values in action. Lead by doing what you say, and make sure you live out your company and team's main values every single day. Embrace them. In the end, it is about practising what you preach and making those values a part of your everyday life. By doing this, you ensure they become an integral part of the company's unique identity.

Leading in this manner means transforming theoretical values into actual behaviours, honouring them and laying the groundwork for a *leadership manifesto*. Think of a *leadership manifesto* as a guide on how leaders within a company should behave. The manifesto's content is firmly grounded in the company's behavioural values, a set of internal principles dictating how leaders (and employees) should conduct themselves daily in pursuit of the organization's mission.

You might wonder, why is there such a need? Well, simply because in case a leader deviates from those values, others should feel empowered to offer open feedback and advice based on what they observe. This prevents senior leaders from speaking poorly to junior team members or not supporting their team on jointly owned projects, for example.

When such situations arise, the *leadership manifesto* enables leaders and employees alike to correct the course. A *leadership manifesto* makes feedback less subjective, basing it on an openly declared expectation on how leaders should behave within the company, whereas the team rules as seen earlier are among team members (Figure 23.5).

Figure 23.5 Scripting the Future: Drafting Your Leadership Manifesto

Beyond that reality check, a *leadership manifesto* can equally be a way to assess performance after a project, meeting or a client contract is finished. It can be used to give each other feedback on how we show up in the work and with each other.

Thinking and acting this way brings forth a more meaningful business. It makes it easier to have a bedrock to help guide decisions when hardship hits. By practising such an open dialogue and feedback loop, it is easier to intervene when drastic actions and talks are required.

24

Say Thank You and Connect at a Human Level

Earning trust, working on values, building co-accountability and co-responsibility will not live long as initiatives unless your people are thanked and recognized. In general, there is a tendency to take things for granted. True, we are all paid to do our jobs. However, we assume that because one is already financially compensated, there is no need to pause, thank and recognize the work at hand or the individual.

We however are not machines (at least not yet!) and therefore we thrive on good feelings and emotions. Our souls crave it, and so do our hearts. Saying thank you and recognizing each achievement will give every individual the wings to fly higher, deliver more and believe in the difference they make.

Be warned, however: Saying thank you at a certain point will not suffice. More will be expected. The promotion that is dreamed of, or the title that has been discussed for years – these promises have to become reality. High performers who work hard expect the next step to come within reasonable deadlines. If this promotion is presently out of reach, it is the responsibility of the company to either make it accessible or clearly communicate that, because of the structure or internal policies, the next step is not reachable within the company.

The worst is when a leader entertains the promotion, knowing that it will never happen. The reality is that at the top of the pyramid, positions become scarce, and there is little room to manoeuvre. Yet people work for recognition. It is human nature.

For some, it will be the financial reward; for others, the title; for others, the public acknowledgement. As a leader, it is about identifying what the driver is for every single member of your team – understanding their *intrinsic motivation*. Once discovered, it is about managing expectations and following up with transparent and clear communication. Transparency should be reciprocal between the employee and the employer.

Tip 1: Spread Happiness in the Workplace

In October 2021, I was interviewed for an article that Cheryl's Cookies had commissioned on the many benefits of saying *thank you*. At that point in my career, I had tried hard to cultivate happiness and flow in the corporate world. The question the writer from Cheryl's Cookies asked me first was: 'Why is saying thank you so important?' My thoughts were rather straightforward. Maybe because it is just about the best gift you can give to someone.

It makes them feel good and will make you feel amazing as well. It is about taking the time to acknowledge and recognize someone's impact on your life. It is about planting the seeds, one after another, to grow a forest of happy human beings. Thinking about it, sending a Thank You is one of my favourite ways of spreading happiness.

This quote is the one that was chosen: 'To say thank you costs nothing, but it gives someone else a positive psychological boost. We live in fast-moving times, but by practicing the act of thanking someone, you can slow things down and appreciate the time and energy the other person has given to you. It is a nice way to be grateful for what you have been given.'

If you do something nice for someone else, how does it make you feel? Spikes of happiness are usually high after sending a thank-you note to someone who deserved your gratitude. In spreading love, happiness, joy and gratitude, you will fill your heart with the same feelings (Figure 24.1). Next time you extend such an act of kindness, pause and reflect on how it made you feel. If it made you feel wonderful, which I suspect it will, replicate this situation as often as you can.

Figure 24.1 The Ripple of Gratitude: Spreading Joy, One Thank You at a Time

Each time a person encounters you and your kindness, that same person may be inspired to do the same. Imagine how powerful such a gesture could become. It could contribute to changing the course of things, in ensuring that as human beings we remember that at the end, all that matters is love and kindness toward ourselves and others.

As a flow leader, when was the last time you thanked your team? And by this, I mean truly taking the time to acknowledge their accomplishments. Trust me, even in the workplace, gratitude is welcome and generates trust.

This quote truly came from my heart and set of beliefs. It must have resonated with Cheryl's Cookies as well: 'A thank-you is a positive extension of your heart out to someone else's heart.' We often take things for granted and forget to look at life with children's eyes or from the perspective of others. Simply by being present, aware and mindful can we notice the needs of others. A simple thank you, if expressed in a thoughtful, authentic and genuine way, can have a profound impact on a person.

Tip 2: Say 'Thank You' Instead of 'I am Sorry'

Saying 'thank you' is the most wonderful antidote to the 'I am sorry' trap. Why? It helps to focus on the positive understanding of the other rather than focusing on what you did that was negative. An apology is a great start. But it may not change the situation, and the risk is that the feeling remains. In the end, the other person may not feel any better.

Thank you, on the other hand, can make everyone feel good regardless of what was done to deserve it. Thank you is in free supply and therefore should be spread in a faster and more meaningful way. Saying 'thank you' is focusing on the other, as opposed to focusing on yourself. It is a fantastic way to give our ego a break and think of others and their impact on our lives.

Writing this section brings me back to my personal stories. Often, my partner will pinpoint something that is beneficial to my growth. When this happens, my first reaction is to fire back, to get angry and to react. It touches something in me, perhaps because he is right. A simple discussion can turn into quite the argument. After I am through being upset, when my anger is gone and peace has returned, I can see things more clearly for what they are.

In the end, the truth can hurt, but instead of getting upset, what I should really be is thankful. Through this exchange, in seeing the situation for what it is and receiving his feedback, he has helped me uncover a new part about myself. To have closure after such an incident, I find that the best course is to acknowledge our own behaviour, take ownership of it and extend a heartfelt 'thank you' for the learning. And yes, it is hard to do. Our egos can make it impossible; however, when such a step is accomplished, it is liberating. (This is still a HUGE work in progress on my end. Hope it will be easier on your end.)

Tip 3: Personalize Your 'Thank You' for Deeper Meaning and Connection

Take it a step further and try to add meaning to your 'thank you'. Reflect on your own knowledge about who the recipient is. When a personalized and genuine 'thank you' is conveyed, the impact is so much greater. It shifts the act from a quick and random exercise to a more meaningful interaction, offering a deeper connection.

- *What do you know about this person?*
- *Do you know their passions, hobbies and centres of interests?*
- *What makes them tick?*
- *What creates the spark and the magic?*
- *What would bring them those fuzzy feelings of being loved and cared for?*

In doing this research, and going through such a thought process, the 'thank you' becomes relevant and personalized. It illustrates that you have truly put your intention into your appreciation.

To say 'thank you' out of the blue is the most surprising delight to someone. And to say it in a meaningful way will create an unexpected moment in time and a long-lasting memory. Saying 'thank you' is a wonderful way to connect and reconnect with others. Oftentimes we hesitate to get back in touch with someone we have not spoken with in years because maybe now we need them. Yet to reconnect and express how grateful you were for what they brought you in your life, even if years later, is a wonderful way to rekindle a relationship – of course, only if this resonates as a true reality.

If you are feeling hesitant because you do not know how your gift or your 'thank you' note will be received, just try it out. The reality is that, by second-guessing yourself, trying to anticipate someone's reaction makes you feel fatigued. To always imagine what people will think rather than to just act can be exhausting. Do not waste more time; as Nike would say: 'Just do it'.

Emotions are contagious. So what about inspiring someone else to say 'thank you' and then starting a chain reaction of spreading good feelings? We can inject positivity into our environment through these first little steps, which in turn can become big strides toward greater happiness for everyone in the workplace. Remember that saying 'thank you' can be applied on the three layers – at the individual, team and organizational level – of the *flow leadership* triangle.

Tip 4: Witness the Act of Caring for Your Teams

This reminds me of a discussion I had with a girl who had just started at the beauty salon I go to. She had just passed her trial period at the salon and was over the moon with joy. That evening, she was in a chatty mood, and we spoke at length.

She told me how much she loved her new work environment and felt inspired by her new boss. Curious, I asked why. Her answers were a textbook approach of what an inspirational leader should be. In a few minutes she recapped why saying 'thank you' matters in the workplace as much as in private circumstances.

She explained how the salon owner leads by example, 'She owns the place, yet she comes in to work with me simply to learn more about me. I feel she cares and is focused on my well-being and growth.'

This young person was delighted. She continued, "At 23 years old, all I want is to grow, learn and add skills to offer more services. Here, she invests in us. She motivates us in showing us the path. In my previous role I was bored, but now I am motivated. And on top of that, she organizes the working hours so the staff can balance out their work life."

And she went on, 'She does not have to, but she wants to.' Working in the service industry is tough with long hours, and she explained how her boss made the difference. 'Here I feel rewarded for it. She tries to give us the days off that we would prefer. She motivates me and gives me confidence that I do a good job. She tells me "thank you". I have never had anyone telling me "thank you" for doing my job. It is expected. Well, not for her.'

In doing so, this leader elevates her team according to my beauty specialist, "It gives me wings. It gives me confidence. It gives me the motivation to want to be a better employee. It makes me want to grow and ask for feedback on how to improve. It makes me feel like I am valued. It gives me the belief that I matter, exist and that I am seen. It shows me that she cares enough to acknowledge my small contribution to her business. For this I am grateful and for this reason she earned my forever loyalty."

Would not you want all your employees to feel that way? I would, having witnessed the outstanding customer experience that this team provides and the passion with which thy work.

Sometimes, no matter what you try to do, it will never be enough for some of your team members. They will want more, rarely giving you solutions to their expectations. Instead, they will show you what is not working. While the feedback is great, and some elements are worth noting, equally know that your role as a leader is not to please everyone. Those team members are most likely looking for a reason to express their frustration, unhappiness and lack of flow. Often, your team members that complain the most are the ones who will leave first, too (Figure 24.2).

The notion of boundaries here is paramount. In doing the work individually and collectively as a team, you will become the mirror of the inner work to be done. While some of your team members will embark on the same journey as you, for some, it may not resonate. And that is okay.

Figure 24.2 Not Everyone's Cup of Tea: Leading Through the Noise

This process will have allowed them to understand their own intrinsic needs. You cannot be everyone's cup of tea. There are many tastes and many flavours. Under such circumstances, the best option is to remain genuine, with an open heart, and encourage the person to walk her or his path, parting on good terms, knowing that you are instigating their growth and yours.

Remember in each situation, good or bad, there is learning, a validation of the action undertaken.

Tip 5: Ask for Your Team's Input

Once during a workshop, a participant asked if we could have an *appreciation box*, and if I thought it would be a good idea. Unsure what she meant, I asked for more details. Her plan was for anyone in the team to submit an appreciation letter anonymously to highlight the work of a fellow team member. This, she felt, would create a positive vibe and allow employees to anonymously say 'thank you' to someone they had worked with. My role was to keep the key to the appreciation box, and my duty would be to check its contents and share the information during our bi-weekly meetings.

This is one of many examples on how happiness can be spread. Expect the box or your initiative to pique the interest of the other departments. Such a small gesture can generate the biggest internal discussion and debate on the power of saying 'thank you' and in recognizing and seeing our employees. The challenging part here is to keep this initiative alive. While the actual practice (anonymous messages) of this particular initiative did not stick, the pure intention behind gratitude and acknowledgement permeated the team and evolved into open dialogue between team members.

Tip 6: Gain the Ability to Connect on a Human-to-Human Level

Casual conversations where you share personal aspects of your life can humanize the dynamic between leaders and teams. This can feel intimidating or like a loss of power for some leaders. You may have fears inside of yourself that are unresolved. If you have gone in to do your personal work, then you are not scared of all these things because you own the space. Why would you fear sharing something that belongs to you? You know that your worth because you are working at it every day.

Of course, everything needs to be done in balance. You are not going to overshare and tell your team everything about your life, but you can give them enough so they can see that you are like them. You are sharing the same reality that they have.

On my end, I talked about my children and hoped to make my team laugh by sharing personal stories, like how after my twin pregnancy, I had to give away all the shoes I had collected over the years because I gained an entire shoe size. Telling them little stories opens them up to having the opportunity to share the same about their lives.

Figure 24.3 Painting the Picture: Opening Windows to Connection

Sometimes we do not do this because we are scared to mix our business and personal lives. In doing so, your team will see you as a human. They will see that there is a window into your life that gives them the opportunity to then speak about themselves and open about certain challenges they are facing (Figure 24.3). It creates a nice – and important – rapport. It humanizes our workplace.

25

Embracing *the Journey*

Flow leadership emanates from within, rooted in deep self-awareness and a profound understanding of oneself. It is not just about external strategies or techniques but about cultivating an inner state of being that naturally inspires and guides others.

Transforming the workplace begins with transforming ourselves. Who we are as individuals profoundly shapes how we lead. Our values, beliefs and behaviours define the type of leader we become. *Flow leadership* is about aligning our inner values with our outward actions, creating a harmonious and authentic leadership style.

Earn trust through authenticity and consistency. Trust is the cornerstone of effective leadership. It is not given; it is earned through our actions and behaviours. Flow leaders prioritize building trust with their teams, creating a safe and empowering environment where people can thrive and contribute their best.

Thankfulness and genuine connections fuel the journey. Acknowledging and appreciating others' efforts is a powerful way to foster a sense of belonging and purpose. Saying 'thank you' and connecting at a human level not only strengthen relationships but also reinforce the values of empathy and appreciation within the organizational culture.

In the journey of *flow leadership*, the 3Ps – *People, Purpose* and *Performance* – serve as guiding principles. Placing people at the centre, aligning actions with a meaningful purpose and focusing on sustainable performance create a holistic approach to leadership that nurtures both individuals and organizations.

We inspire to be inspired, leading a ripple effect of greatness. Leadership extends beyond titles; it is about inspiring others to reach their full potential. Every individual has the power to inspire and uplift those around them (Figure 25.1).

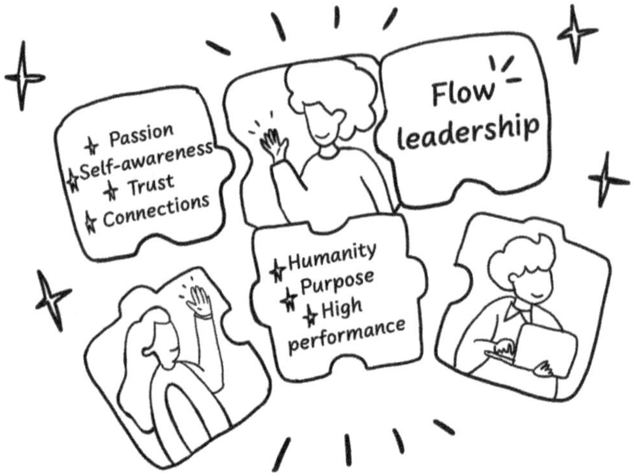

Figure 25.1 Pieces of Inspiration: Assembling a Ripple of Greatness

In closing, I invite you to embrace the journey of *flow leadership* with purpose and passion. Let the pursuit of self-awareness, trust-building and authentic connections guide your path.

As leaders collectively shift towards placing *people* back at the centre of the equation, may each one of us feel inspired to inspire others, knowing that together, we can create a workplace culture that values humanity, purpose and high performance – a culture where everyone can thrive and contribute to a brighter future.

26

The Seeds of Change

Flow Leadership is about understanding the delicate balance between the 3Ps – *People, Purpose* and *Performance*. It is not about directing people, tasks or projects. It is about inspiring minds and hearts. An effective leader always invests in *people* first, empowering them to find FLOW@WORK.

Place your *people*'s well-being at the forefront of your strategies. Guide them to *purpose* and *performance*. Make it a point that caring leadership does not take away from success and performance. On the contrary, it fosters expansion (Figure 26.1).

Figure 26.1 The Seeds of Change 1: Illuminating Growth – Unlocking FLOW@WORK

Working hard, being commercially driven and caring for the well-being of your people can coexist in a healthy workplace. Meritocracy still exists. Stick to your values. Show up for both your people and yourself.

Creating an open dialogue will help you form a plan on how to find FLOW@WORK, individually and as a team. Once you start this journey, it will become a regular pit stop. Assess (ideally quarterly) how the plan is coming along. By checking in, you will be able to see the stages your employees are at in their own journey.

And for those who remain sceptical, thinking that they are already doing enough, my question is very simple:

Are you sure this is the case?

If you were truly serving your *people,* would the corporate key performance indicators still look the same as they do today? KPIs have not changed; they are the same archaic KPIs whose main purpose is to serve the system. Yet the world *has* changed, and so have your people.

Isn't it time to change those outdated KPIs and focus on the well-being of your people?

Simply put, rethinking how we treat people is the only way to truly put them first. Allow them to be happy and find their FLOW@WORK.

Start walking the path of your *people* because your products or services will not sell by themselves. Your brand will be a logo on paper, and your strategies nothing more than beautiful PowerPoint presentations. Brands and organizations are made of ***people***; *people* buy from *people. People* need *purpose* to create impact.

Give them that *purpose*, that meaning, and create social value and capital that support their well-being and happiness for enhanced *performance*.

Embracing the power of the 3Ps can lead to a workplace where flow becomes a natural and transformative state. Aren't we all spiritual beings having a human experience at work? Aware or not, don't we crave to be in a good place to be in our flow?

Imagine a motivated workforce, creative, happy and stress-free, capable in their flow of withstanding any challenges, united in times of need. It could become *your* reality. And *you* can make the difference (Figure 26.2).

Plant the seeds of change!

Figure 26.2 The Seeds of Change 2: Plant the Seeds of Change

Part IV

Key Takeaways

19 **Transform the Workplace by Transforming Yourself**

- Recognize that true leadership goes beyond formal education and requires internal reflection and growth.
- Develop greater empathy and insight into how your actions impact others through external awareness.
- Lead by example and align your actions with your core values, establishing credibility and trust among your team members.

FlowBite: *Flow leadership starts from within.*

20 ***Flow Leadership*** **Comes from Self-Awareness**

Tip 1: 'Self-check-in' to become self-aware

- Tune into yourself to improve your ability to give and lead effectively.
- Identify your triggers as reactions often stem from unresolved internal issues.

FlowBite: *Tune into yourself to lead effectively.*

Tip 2: Identify and transcend 'cognitive dissonance'.

- Recognize the prevalence of cognitive dissonance in the workplace in tackling mental frictions to align thoughts and actions.
- Prioritize mental immunity to improve effectiveness and resilience as a leader.

- Understand introspection, your brain's ability to monitor thoughts and responses, for better leadership outcomes.

FlowBite: *Cultivate and form habits through introspection.*

Tip 3: Openly share your 'to work on' list.

- Demonstrate self-awareness and personal development to encourage team cohesion and performance.
- Utilize a 'to work on' list to encourage open sharing and vulnerability to foster a culture of personal growth within your team.

FlowBite: *Embrace feedback for continuous growth.*

Tip 4: Recondition your beliefs.

- Manage emotions through self-regulation by trying to understand and accepting your own emotions as well as those of your people for better interactions.
- Leverage strong social skills effectively and ensure clear communication for resolving conflicts and misunderstandings.

FlowBite: *Reshape the world of leadership with social awareness.*

21 Who You Are Is How You Lead

Tip 1: From self-awareness to external awareness – understand your impact on others

- Prioritize empathy in leadership to connect emotionally with team members and enhance team resilience.
- Foster external awareness to better understand how your behaviour impacts your team.

- Practice active listening and pay attention to non-verbal cues to deepen your understanding of your team's experiences.

FlowBite: *Cultivate emotional intelligence and conscious leadership.*

Tip 2: *People* before paperwork and process

- Understand the difference between empathy and sympathy to connect at an emotional level, not just feeling sorry for someone.
- Focus on gaining others' perspectives, first, to further cultivate empathy.

FlowBite: *Embrace empathy as a critical skill: it is important for all business leaders, not just HR professionals.*

22 Earn Your *People*'s Trust

Tip 1: Stand up for your team

- Prioritize building trust in leadership by modelling the expected behaviour and demonstrating the values and actions you expect from your team members.
- Take ownership and accountability – support and stand up for your team members.

FlowBite: *Advocate actively and stand in solidarity, leadership demands more than supervision; it requires active support and unity.*

Tip 2: Create co-responsibility and co-accountability

- Define co-accountability and co-responsibility by setting clear rules and expectations within the team to promote ownership.

- Help your employees understand their responsibilities and the impact and value of their contributions.
- Set high standards and clear expectations to encourage a culture of excellence and self-accountability among team members.

FlowBite: *Break the cycle of co-dependency – enable team members to take ownership and pride in their work.*

23 From Theoretical Values to a Behavioural Set of Principles

Tip 1: Navigate the world of values

- Establish a mutual understanding of core values – personal, team and organization.
- Foster a culture of values-driven decision-making to guide behaviour and shape the organizational culture.
- Incorporate values into daily practices to ensure alignment with organizational goals and mission.

FlowBite: *Learn how to navigate the world of values.*

Tip 2: Examine how your values have permeated the organization

- Assess values clarity and alignment layer by layer starting with individuals (*people*), then teams, and finally the overarching company.
- Increase alignment to reduce resistance to enhance the transformation of theoretical values into behavioural ones.

FlowBite: *Activate your values within your leadership philosophy.*

Tip 3: Raise the awareness on your company values

- Create a compelling story and make your values exciting and visible inside and outside the workplace.

- Integrate core values into your company's communication strategy.

FlowBite: *Act as the guardian of your company values.*

Tip 4: From brand values to service philosophy

- Develop a *service philosophy*, a framework for employees to live and embody company values in their daily work.
- Integrate values into job roles to ensure that every employee understands their role in reflecting company values.

FlowBite: *Live and service by your company values.*

Tip 5: Practice what you preach!

- Demonstrate values through action by being authentic and true to yourself as a flow leader.
- Establish a *leadership manifesto*, a guide outlining how leaders should behave based on the company's behavioural values.
- Ensure that the manifesto reflects the internal principles guiding leaders and employees in achieving the organization's mission.

FlowBite: *Call yourself and others out when values are not respected.*

24 Say Thank You and Connect at a Human Level

Tip 1: Spread Happiness in the workplace

- Appreciate that meaningful recognition entails understanding what drives each team member.
- Reflect on how acts of kindness and gratitude elevate your own happiness.

- Inspire a chain reaction and witness the power of your actions in inspiring others to reciprocate kindness and gratitude.

FlowBite: *Build trust through gratitude and foster a culture of appreciation.*

Tip 2: Say 'thank you' instead of 'I am sorry'

- Highlight the positive impact of saying 'thank you' compared to focusing solely on apologies.
- Recognize that expressing gratitude can uplift spirits and create a more positive atmosphere.

FlowBite: *Shift focus to positivity; encourage a mindset that focuses on understanding and appreciation rather than dwelling on negativity.*

Tip 3: Personalize your 'thank you' for deeper meaning and connection

- Shift from routine expressions to meaningful interactions that foster deeper connections and memorable moments.
- Surprise and delight with spontaneous and thoughtful 'thank you' gestures to pleasantly surprise and uplift individuals.

FlowBite: *Cultivate connection through gratitude; use gratitude as a tool to connect and reconnect with others on a personal and meaningful level.*

Tip 4: Witness the act of caring for your teams

- Stay true to yourself and lead with an open heart, acknowledging that not everyone will align with your leadership style or decisions.

- Emphasize the value of each experience, whether positive or challenging, as opportunities for personal and professional development.
- Understand that not everyone will be satisfied despite efforts; focus on genuine leadership rather than pleasing everyone.

FlowBite: *Recognize inspirational leadership qualities; identify traits that inspire and motivate individuals within a work environment.*

Tip 5: Ask your team for input

- Foster appreciation and recognition by implementing initiatives to encourage team members to acknowledge and celebrate each other's contributions.
- Be flexible and open to changes in how appreciation is expressed, recognizing that different approaches may resonate more with team dynamics over time.
- Sustain efforts to promote appreciation and recognition by consistently reinforcing the value of expressing gratitude within the team.

FlowBite: *Foster a culture of recognition and mutual respect; encourage verbal acknowledgement.*

Tip 6: Gain the ability to connect on a human-to-human level

- Open a window into your life by acknowledging potential discomfort or power concerns and emphasize the value of humanizing interactions.
- Cultivate a positive and supportive atmosphere through genuine interactions and mutual understanding.

- Promote a culture where individuals feel valued, heard and connected beyond professional roles, enhancing overall workplace dynamics.

FlowBite: *Humanize leadership dynamics; foster casual conversations and connect on a human level with your team.*

25 Embracing *the Journey*

- Cultivate inner self-awareness: *Flow leadership* starts with a deep understanding of oneself and inner values.
- Align inner values with actions: Authentic leadership stems from harmonizing personal values with outward behaviours.
- Earn trust through consistency: Build trust by demonstrating authenticity and consistency in actions and decisions.
- Foster genuine connections: Appreciate and connect with others on a human level to strengthen relationships and organizational culture.
- Inspire and uplift others: Lead by inspiring individuals to reach their full potential and contribute positively to the organization.
- Pursue *purpose* and passion: Embrace the journey of *flow leadership* with *purpose* and passion, focusing on self-awareness, trust-building and authentic connections.

FlowBite: *Shift towards human-centric leadership; encourage a workplace culture that values humanity, purpose and high performance for a brighter future.*

Appendix: The FLOW@WORK Research Survey

FLOW@WORK Survey V2

Welcome to the FLOW@WORK™ Leadership Survey

Thank you for participating in the **FLOW@WORK™ Leadership Survey.** This survey is a vital part of our ongoing efforts to evaluate and enhance the key components of our leadership culture, specifically focusing on the 3Ps: *People, Purpose* and *Performance*. Your insights will help us understand how effectively we are fostering an environment where team members feel valued, aligned with a clear purpose and empowered to perform at their highest potential.

This survey is owned and managed by **FLOW@WORK™**, and all the information collected will remain secure and confidential, used exclusively to improve our organizational culture and practices. If you have any questions or concerns about the survey, feel free to reach out to us at info@gaelledevins.com.

By clicking "I consent," you agree to participate in this survey.

Before You Begin

- Time Commitment: The survey will take approximately 10 to 15 minutes to complete.

- Confidentiality: All responses are confidential and will be used in aggregate to improve our organizational practices. Your honest feedback is invaluable in shaping an environment that supports growth and engagement for everyone.

Instructions

- Please respond to each question openly and honestly based on your personal experience.
- There are no "right" or "wrong" answers – we are interested in your genuine insights and perspectives.
- A progress indicator will be displayed to help you track your completion as you move through the survey.

Why Your Input Matters

Your feedback is instrumental in helping us achieve the right balance between *People, Purpose* and *Performance.* By sharing your experiences, you are contributing to our collective goal of creating a workplace where everyone thrives – where individuals are supported, teams are aligned with meaningful goals, and high performance is both achievable and sustainable. Thank you for taking the time to share your insights on how we can build a more purpose-driven, engaged and high-performing organization.

Demographics

Introduction to Demographics:

To better understand our participants, we have a few questions that are solely for classification purposes. Answers will be kept anonymous.

1. What is your gender identity?
    1. Male
    2. Female
    3. Non-binary
    4. Prefer not to answer
2. What is your age?
    1. 18–24
    2. 25–39
    3. 40–56
    4. 57–75
    5. 76 or older
    6. Prefer not to answer
3. What is your current job level or position?
    1. Entry level
    2. Mid-level
    3. Senior level
    4. Executive/leadership
    5. Prefer not to answer
4. How long have you been employed with the company?
    1. Less than 6 months
    2. 6 months to 1 year
    3. 1–3 years
    4. 3–5 years
    5. 5–10 years
    6. More than 10 years
    7. Prefer not to answer

5. Please indicate in which of the following categories you would place yourself.
    1. White or Caucasian
    2. Black or African
    3. Latino or Hispanic
    4. Asian
    5. Mixed race
    6. Middle Eastern
    7. Other

Section 1: *People (P1)*

People represent the workforce's emotional connection, engagement and collaboration. Leadership's role is to foster an environment where employees feel valued and supported, driving flow experiences. Please rate the following statements from 1 to 5, where 1 means 'strongly disagree', 3 is 'neutral' and 5 means 'strongly agree'.

1. My direct leader actively promotes a sense of belonging and emotional connection within the team.
    1. Strongly disagree
    2. Disagree
    3. Neutral
    4. Agree
    5. Strongly agree
2. I feel my contributions are valued and recognized by my team and organization.
    1. Strongly disagree
    2. Disagree
    3. Neutral
    4. Agree
    5. Strongly agree

3. I regularly collaborate with my team members in a way that makes me feel energized and engaged with the team.
   1. Strongly disagree
   2. Disagree
   3. Neutral
   4. Agree
   5. Strongly agree
4. In my team, we effectively communicate and respect each other's emotions and perspectives.
   1. Strongly disagree
   2. Disagree
   3. Neutral
   4. Agree
   5. Strongly agree
5. I feel a deep sense of fulfilment and personal growth in my role.
   1. Strongly disagree
   2. Disagree
   3. Neutral
   4. Agree
   5. Strongly agree
6. I feel that my strengths and talents are recognized and supported by my team and leader.
   1. Strongly disagree
   2. Disagree
   3. Neutral
   4. Agree
   5. Strongly agree

7. I feel empowered to take initiative and contribute beyond my immediate tasks.
    1. Strongly disagree
    2. Disagree
    3. Neutral
    4. Agree
    5. Strongly agree
8. My team members and I support each other through challenges and ensure a positive, collaborative environment.
    1. Strongly disagree
    2. Disagree
    3. Neutral
    4. Agree
    5. Strongly agree

Open-ended question: What do you believe your team or leadership could do better to help you feel more engaged and supported at work?

Section 2: *Purpose (P2)*

Purpose is about aligning individual and team goals with the organization's broader mission. Leadership ensures employees understand and connect with the organization's purpose, driving motivation and flow. Please rate the following statements from 1 to 5, where 1 means 'strongly disagree', 3 is 'neutral' and 5 means 'strongly agree'.

1. I clearly understand how my role contributes to the organization's broader goals.
    1. Strongly disagree
    2. Disagree
    3. Neutral
    4. Agree
    5. Strongly agree
2. The work I do aligns with my personal values and what I believe in.
    1. Strongly disagree
    2. Disagree
    3. Neutral
    4. Agree
    5. Strongly agree
3. I feel that my work contributes to a higher purpose beyond just financial outcomes.
    1. Strongly disagree
    2. Disagree
    3. Neutral
    4. Agree
    5. Strongly agree
4. The company's mission and values are clearly communicated and guide our work.
    1. Strongly disagree
    2. Disagree
    3. Neutral
    4. Agree
    5. Strongly agree

5. I am motivated by the purpose and goals of my team.
    1. Strongly disagree
    2. Disagree
    3. Neutral
    4. Agree
    5. Strongly agree
6. I derive a sense of meaning from the impact my work has on others, both within and outside the organization.
    1. Strongly disagree
    2. Disagree
    3. Neutral
    4. Agree
    5. Strongly agree
7. My team's objectives align with the company's purpose, and this clarity drives our collective efforts.
    1. Strongly disagree
    2. Disagree
    3. Neutral
    4. Agree
    5. Strongly agree
8. I feel that my work supports a purpose that is greater than just day-to-day tasks or immediate goals.
    1. Strongly disagree
    2. Disagree
    3. Neutral
    4. Agree
    5. Strongly agree

Open-ended question: Is there a part of the company's mission or purpose that particularly motivates or inspires you? If so, why?

Section 3: *Performance (P3)*

Performance relates to balancing challenges with skills. Leadership must ensure that employees' abilities match the tasks, driving continuous improvement and enabling flow experiences. Please rate the following statements from 1 to 5, where 1 means 'strongly disagree', 3 is 'neutral' and 5 means 'strongly agree'.

1. The tasks I work on are challenging but aligned with my skills and capabilities.
    1. Strongly disagree
    2. Disagree
    3. Neutral
    4. Agree
    5. Strongly agree
2. I feel equipped with the necessary skills, tools and resources to meet my job's challenges.
    1. Strongly disagree
    2. Disagree
    3. Neutral
    4. Agree
    5. Strongly agree
3. The work I do is appropriately challenging and allows me to stretch my skills without becoming overwhelmed.
    1. Strongly disagree
    2. Disagree
    3. Neutral
    4. Agree
    5. Strongly agree

4. I consistently receive feedback that helps me improve my performance.
   1. Strongly disagree
   2. Disagree
   3. Neutral
   4. Agree
   5. Strongly agree
5. My team and I are always looking for ways to improve our performance and reach new levels of productivity.
   1. Strongly disagree
   2. Disagree
   3. Neutral
   4. Agree
   5. Strongly agree
6. I feel encouraged to take risks, experiment and innovate in my role to improve our team's performance.
   1. Strongly disagree
   2. Disagree
   3. Neutral
   4. Agree
   5. Strongly agree
7. Our team regularly reviews our goals and adjusts them to stay aligned with performance expectations.
   1. Strongly disagree
   2. Disagree
   3. Neutral
   4. Agree
   5. Strongly agree

8. I am provided with clear, actionable feedback that helps me improve my performance on a regular basis.
    1. Strongly disagree
    2. Disagree
    3. Neutral
    4. Agree
    5. Strongly agree

Open-ended question: What is the biggest challenge you currently face in your role, and how could the organization better support you in overcoming it?

Section 4: *Multidimensional People Scale*

The multidimensional people scale is a 22-item construct that has been developed to examine and understand the nuances of people's organizational needs. This scale will enable us to test to what extent each facet contributes to people and the overall FLOW@WORK model.

Please rate the following statements from 1 to 5, where 1 means 'strongly disagree', 3 is 'neutral' and 5 means 'strongly agree'.

1. My organization provides a safe and secure work environment.
    1. Strongly disagree
    2. Disagree
    3. Neutral
    4. Agree
    5. Strongly agree

2. I am confident in the stability of my employment here.
    1. Strongly disagree
    2. Disagree
    3. Neutral
    4. Agree
    5. Strongly agree
3. I am happy with my current salary.
    1. Strongly disagree
    2. Disagree
    3. Neutral
    4. Agree
    5. Strongly agree
4. My compensation is fair and aligns with the responsibilities of my role.
    1. Strongly disagree
    2. Disagree
    3. Neutral
    4. Agree
    5. Strongly agree
5. I feel a strong sense of belonging within my team.
    1. Strongly disagree
    2. Disagree
    3. Neutral
    4. Agree
    5. Strongly agree
6. My organization makes me feel welcome and accepted.
    1. Strongly disagree
    2. Disagree
    3. Neutral
    4. Agree
    5. Strongly agree

7. I feel valued as an individual by my colleagues and supervisors.
    1. Strongly disagree
    2. Disagree
    3. Neutral
    4. Agree
    5. Strongly agree
8. I have the flexibility to make decisions in my role.
    1. Strongly disagree
    2. Disagree
    3. Neutral
    4. Agree
    5. Strongly agree
9. I am able to manage my workload in a way that suits me.
    1. Strongly disagree
    2. Disagree
    3. Neutral
    4. Agree
    5. Strongly agree
10. I have ownership over the projects for which I am responsible.
    1. Strongly disagree
    2. Disagree
    3. Neutral
    4. Agree
    5. Strongly agree

11. My organization provides opportunities for me to develop my skills.
    1. Strongly disagree
    2. Disagree
    3. Neutral
    4. Agree
    5. Strongly agree
12. I receive constructive feedback that helps me improve professionally.
    1. Strongly disagree
    2. Disagree
    3. Neutral
    4. Agree
    5. Strongly agree
13. There are clear pathways for advancement in my role.
    1. Strongly disagree
    2. Disagree
    3. Neutral
    4. Agree
    5. Strongly agree
14. The work I do aligns with my personal values.
    1. Strongly disagree
    2. Disagree
    3. Neutral
    4. Agree
    5. Strongly agree
15. I feel that my contributions make a meaningful impact.
    1. Strongly disagree
    2. Disagree
    3. Neutral
    4. Agree
    5. Strongly agree

16. My organization's values align with my values.
    1. Strongly disagree
    2. Disagree
    3. Neutral
    4. Agree
    5. Strongly agree
17. I am recognized for my accomplishments at work.
    1. Strongly disagree
    2. Disagree
    3. Neutral
    4. Agree
    5. Strongly agree
18. My organization celebrates and rewards high performance.
    1. Strongly disagree
    2. Disagree
    3. Neutral
    4. Agree
    5. Strongly agree
19. I feel a sense of accomplishment from reaching my goals.
    1. Strongly disagree
    2. Disagree
    3. Neutral
    4. Agree
    5. Strongly agree
20. My role allows me to explore new ideas and be creative.
    1. Strongly disagree
    2. Disagree
    3. Neutral
    4. Agree
    5. Strongly agree

21. I am able to work on projects that reflect my personal passions.
    1. Strongly disagree
    2. Disagree
    3. Neutral
    4. Agree
    5. Strongly agree
22. I feel that I am growing and reaching my potential in this organization.
    1. Strongly disagree
    2. Disagree
    3. Neutral
    4. Agree
    5. Strongly agree

Acknowledgements

Thank you to my partner, **Chance Newcombe-Bilham**, for making my dream of becoming a mother come true. He showed me what love and partnership really mean. He believed in me and encouraged me to write this book when no one else did. This book is thanks to him.

To my dear twins, **Athena and Oliver**: you gave me the greatest gift before you were even born: the strength to follow my dream. How could I tell you to chase your dreams if I did not chase mine? Together, we began this journey – when you danced in my belly at night, I was writing. Later, as you slept in your cribs, I kept going. You inspired me to be stronger and better. Thank you for giving me purpose and joy.

To my dear parents, **mother and father (les Devins)**: you have always been my rock. Once again, you supported me wholeheartedly, even rallying behind this crazy idea of mine. You asked for a French translation before the book was even published – maybe one day, just for you. Your love, support and the life you gave me made this book possible. Whether it finds success or not, I dedicate it to you with all my heart. Thank you.

To my brother (Gaëtan Devins): you hold a special place in my heart, and I am so blessed to have you as a pillar in my life. I have always admired you – for finding true love, building a beautiful family and becoming a successful COO while keeping your kindness and generosity.

From the moment I shared this book idea, you showed genuine interest and unwavering support. Thank you for believing in me and proving that even a rational mind can embrace this message. Your faith gave me hope it could resonate with others.

To my dear editors, **Jacqueline Rupp and Paulin Prifti**: you were my fearless cheerleaders alongside Chance. From the very beginning, you were in my corner, helping me bring this book to life. I will never forget the day I handed you my manuscript in tears, doubting everything. Your wisdom comforted me, and your patience, guidance and encouragement gave me the strength to believe in my message. Thank you for helping me see this journey through.

To my talented illustrator, **Mina Yanci**: thank you for bringing the business concepts in this book to life through your incredible illustrations. Your talent and kindness shone through every step, synthesizing the content and capturing the essence of each idea. As the saying goes, pictures speak 10,000 words, and your work speaks volumes, carrying deep emotions and enhancing the message of this book. You poured your heart into this project, and it shows. I could not have asked for better partners.

To **Dr Bashar Albaghli**: thank you for guiding me through the research – a field I was not familiar with, especially when it came to correlations, regression analysis and statistical modelling. Working with you made it possible not only to refine my book concept but also to navigate and understand this domain, one step at a time. Perhaps true genius is making the complex seem simple, and you did exactly that. Part III of this book exists because of your expertise, support and research findings. Thank you for being an essential part of this journey.

To **Martin Gonzalez, Cheryl Segura and Annie Knight**: thank you for being the miracle chain that made my dream come true. For four long years, I struggled to get my book published. I pushed, I persisted, but nothing happened. Then, one person changed everything. It began with Martin, who asked his agent a simple question. That one act led me to Cheryl, who introduced me to Annie. In just ten days, everything fell into place. Suddenly, the dream that had felt so distant became a reality. I signed a contract with **Wiley**, and it felt like magic. What made it truly special was not just the result but the people behind it. Each of you cared deeply and genuinely. You wanted to help, and your kindness carried me through. I still remember that night. I was on a rare getaway with my partner Chance Newcombe-Bilham, preparing for a pre-dinner drink. I could not sleep. Even though I wanted to sleep in the next morning, I was wide awake at dawn. Why? Because the book contract had just arrived. It felt bigger than any meeting or business deal I had ever had – a moment of pure joy and gratitude. To Martin, for starting the chain. To Cheryl, for opening the door. To Annie, for making it happen. This book exists because of you, and I will forever be grateful.

To **Georges Kern**: I owe so much of my career to you. In 2011, you gave me my first opportunity in the watchmaking industry. Twelve years later, you brought me along on another exciting adventure with you at **Breitling**. Your loyalty, fairness and belief in me have been a guiding force throughout my journey. You are not just a mentor but a leader and CEO whose vision and drive have always set you apart. When I shared my book project and asked you to write the foreword, you responded with a big smile, 'Okay, Gaëlle, I will do it.' That moment filled me with pride and gratitude – a true reflection of your unwavering support and encouragement over the years. Thank you for your leadership, for believing in my potential and for allowing me to release this book while working for Breitling. Your influence is woven into every page of this book, and for that, I will always be grateful.

To my dearest friends **Christine Auh and Stav Martens**: I am deeply grateful for your invaluable contributions to this book. Your thoughtful challenges to the content, your role as a sounding board and your meticulous editing have made a profound impact. Your dedication and the time you invested have shaped this book in ways I could never have achieved alone. Thank you for believing in me and for making such a meaningful difference.

To my incredible **FlowSquad**: thank you for sticking with me through the years. You have seen my strengths and weaknesses, and yet, you have always stayed close. We have worked together, grown together and somehow managed to keep in touch despite life's twists and turns. Your unwavering support during this book journey has meant the world to me. Thank you for being my strength, my cheerleaders and my constant source of inspiration. This book would not have been the same without you.

To the **remarkable individuals who endorsed** this book: thank you for your generosity, wisdom and belief in my work. You are mentors and role models I deeply admire, and turning to you after completing the first draft was both humbling and nerve-wracking. Despite your accomplishments and busy lives, you did not turn me away. Instead, you embraced this project with open hearts and offered your thoughtful support. Your encouragement gave me the confidence to share this book with the world.

Thank you for lending your voices to amplify its message and for showing me the true power of kindness and mentorship. I am forever grateful.

To my **dear colleagues and teams, both past and present:** from the bottom of my heart, I would like to express my gratitude. Thank you for passionately working with me, entertaining my crazy ideas, and not only listening to them but equally being willing to test them out. None of this would have been possible without you. You are the change-makers, the ones that have carried me along the way. Thank you for taking a chance on me. I am forever grateful for the experiences we shared along the way and all the memories we created. Those magical moments in time will forever stay in my heart and nurture my soul whenever I am in doubt. You have shown me the power of working together and what it feels like to be in flow.

To my dear **Luigi**: your guidance and mentorship have made a difference. With you on my side, my confidence grew daily, allowing me to ask any questions that arose along the way. Empowered by fresh knowledge, I felt ready to move forward. Your professional story gave me the motivation and belief that dreams can happen, regardless of what age or stage of life you are in. You showed me that it is never too late to make the impossible possible. You are remembered and forever in my heart. May you continue to shine your bright light on other stars.

To all my **friends** who showed interest in my project, and most importantly, for the ones who did not really believe or express any interest. It was this lack of belief that gave me even more motivation to pursue this journey. It fuelled my passion and motivation to inspire others to always go after their dreams and listen to their inner voice regardless of what others say.

And most importantly, thank YOU, dear **readers and strangers,** for having given me your time and the benefit of the doubt when picking up this book.

May you chase your dream, find your flow and live with purpose.

Bibliography

Part II: Purpose

Bartimote, H. 28 October 2022. *Five Key Questions to Diagnose a Sick Organization*. Retrieved 11 July 2024: https://blog.container-solutions.com/five-key-questions-to-diagnose-a-sick-organisation

Csikszentmihalyi, M. 1900 New York Harper and Row. *Flow: The Psychology of Optimal Experience*. 15 pp.

Dhingra, N., Andrew, S., Bill, S., & Schrimper, M. 5 April 2021. *Help your employees find purpose – or watch them leave*. Retrieved 12 July 2024: https://www.mckinsey.com/capabilities/people-and-organizational-performance/our-insights/help-your-employees-find-purpose-or-watch-them-leave

Ganesan, K. 19 April 2024. *Importance of employee satisfaction: Why it matters in today's work culture*. Retrieved 12 July 2024: https://www.culturemonkey.io/employee-engagement/importance-of-employee-satisfaction/

Goleman, D. More Than Sound LLC (2nd edition 12 April 2011). *The Brain and Emotional Intelligence: New Insights*.

Goleman, D. for Greater Good Science Center. 20 January 2014. *Focus, Flow, & Frazzle*. Retrieved 03 July 2024: https://www.youtube.com/watch?v=Nexy76Jtu24

Karpenkova, A. 15 February 2022. *What is Organization Health? 6 Pillars of a Health Organization (2024)*. Retrieved 11 July 2024: https://whatfix.com/blog/organizational-health/#:~:text=Organizational%20health%20determines%20a%20company's,maintaining%20a%20highly%20engaged%20workforce

Kotler, S. for Big Think. May 2022. *How to enter 'flow state' on command*. Retrieved 02 July 2024: https://www.youtube.com/watch?v=znwUCNrjpD4

McLennan, Marsh Agency. 14 June 2024. *A complete guide to employee satisfaction in today's workplace*. Retrieved 12 July 2024: https://www.marshmma.com/us/insights/details/employee-satisfaction.html

Mcleod, A. WHIN Monthly Bulletin. Purdue University. *Sick or Healthy Companies: Measure & Fix Work Schedule*. Retrieved 11 July 2024: https://business.purdue.edu/centers/dcmme/engagement/newsletters/sick-or-healthy-companies.php

MindTools Content Team. *Brainwriting*. Retrieved 12 July 2024: https://www.mindtools.com/ak3qj17/brainwriting

Schuyler, S. June 2016. *Putting Purpose to Work: A study of purpose in the workplace*. Retrieved 02 July 2024: https://www.pwc.com/us/en/about-us/corporate-responsibility/assets/pwc-putting-purpose-to-work-purpose-survey-report.pdf

Turner, J. 29 March 2023. *Employee Seek Personal Value and Purpose at Work. Be Prepared to Deliver*. Retrieved 11 July 2024: https://www.gartner.com/en/articles/employees-seek-personal-value-and-purpose-at-work-be-prepared-to-deliver

Wikipedia. Retrieved 02 July 2024: https://en.wikipedia.org/wiki/Flow_(psychology)

Wooll, M. 4 October 2021. *Find the purpose of work by creation purpose in your work*. Retrieved 12 July 2024: https://www.betterup.com/blog/purpose-of-work

Part IV: The Flow Leader

Balconi, M., Angioletti, L., & Crivelli, D. (2020). Neuro-empowerment of executive functions in the workplace: The reason why. *Frontiers in Psychology*, *11*, 1519. https://doi.org/10.3389/fpsyg.2020.01519

Bariso, Justin. Inc.com. 19 September 2018. *There are actually 3 Types of Empathy. Here's How They Differ – and How You Can Develop Them All*. Retrieved 03 July 2024: https://www.inc.com/justin-bariso/there-are-actually-3-types-of-empathy-heres-how-they-differ-and-how-you-can-develop-them-all.html

Bergner, S., Rybnicek, R., & Koschutnig, K. (2022). Leadership and credition: Followers' neural response to leaders who are perceived as transformational. *Frontiers in Behavioral Neuroscience*, *16*, 943896. https://doi.org/10.3389/fnbeh.2022.943896

Callahan, C. Worklife. 9 November 2022. Why empathy is important between generations at work. Retrieved 03 July 2024: https://www.worklife.news/culture/empathy-at-work

Coronado-Maldonado, I., & Benítez-Márquez, M. D. (2023). Emotional intelligence, leadership, and work teams: A hybrid literature review. *Heliyon*, *9*(10), e20356. https://doi.org/10.1016/j.heliyon.2023.e20356

Coronado-Maldonado, I., & Benitez-Marquez, M.-D. National Library of Medicine. *Emotional intelligence, leadership, and work teams: A hybrid literature review*. Retrieved 03 July 2024: https://www.ncbi.nlm.nih.gov/pmc/articles/PMC10543214/

Edelson, M. G., Polania, R., Ruff, C. C., Fehr, E., & Hare, T. A. (2018). Computational and neurobiological foundations of leadership decisions. *Science (New York, N.Y.)*, *361*(6401), eaat0036. https://doi.org/10.1126/science.aat0036

Goleman, D. and Boyatzis, R. E. Harvard Business Review. *Social Intelligence and the Biology of Leadership*. September 2008. Retrieved 03 July 2024: https://hbr.org/2008/09/social-intelligence-and-the-biology-of-leadership

Kumar, S. National Library of Medicine. Jan-June 2014. Establishing linkages between emotional intelligence and transformational leadership. Retrieved 03 July 2024: https://www.ncbi.nlm.nih.gov/pmc/articles/PMC4261205/

Martos, M. P., Lopez-Zafra, E., Pulido-Martos, M., & Augusto, J. M. (2013). Are emotional intelligent workers also more empathic?. *Scandinavian Journal of Psychology*, *54*(5), 407–414. https://doi.org/10.1111/sjop.12058

Platt, M. L. December 2020. Wharton@Work. *The Leader's Brain*. Retrieved 03 July 2024: https://executiveeducation.wharton.upenn.edu/thought-leadership/wharton-at-work/2020/12/michael-platt-the-leaders-brain/

Reshetnikov, V. A., Tvorogova, N. D., Hersonskiy, I. I., Sokolov, N. A., Petrunin, A. D., & Drobyshev, D. A. (2020). Leadership and emotional intelligence: Current trends in public health professionals training. *Frontiers in Public Health*, 7, 413. https://doi.org/10.3389/fpubh.2019.00413

Ruiz-Rodríguez, R., Ortiz-de-Urbina-Criado, M., & Ravina-Ripoll, R. (2023). Neuroleadership: A new way for happiness management. *Humanities & Social Sciences Communications*, *10*(1), 139. https://doi.org/10.1057/s41599-023-01642-w

Stein, S. J. and Book, H. E. Third Edition 2020. THEEQEDGE Emotional Intelligence and your Success. Retrieved 03 July 2024: https://books.google.ch/books?id=aBWCsj63t5YC&printsec=frontcover&dq=&redir_esc=y#v=onepage&q&f=false

Tait, B. 22 April 2020. *Understanding The Neuroscience Behind Emotional Intelligence*. Retrieved 03 July 2024: https://www.forbes.com/sites/forbescoachescouncil/2020/04/22/understanding-the-neuroscience-behind-emotional-intelligence/

Williams, J. A. Heartmanity's Blog. *The Three Kinds of Empathy: Emotional, Cognitive, Compassionate*. Retrieved 03 July 2024: https://blog.heartmanity.com/the-three-kinds-of-empathy-emotional-cognitive-compassionate#:~:text=The%20three%20types%20of%20empathy,by%20social%20and%20cognitive%20psychologists

About the Author

All my life, I have carried a deep desire to make a positive difference to others. It is more than just a wish – it is a need, a calling that fills my heart. If I had a magic wand, I would use it to heal minds, lift spirits and bring joy and well-being to everyone I meet.

Over time, this drive blended with my work. I discovered that leading teams was the perfect way for me to fulfil my purpose. Leadership, for me, is not about being in charge – it is about serving. It is about creating an environment where individuals feel seen, heard and valued.

Watching people and teams surpass their limits fills my workdays with purpose, turning tasks into something meaningful. Leadership is a powerful way to care for others and be part of something greater than myself. That is why every day feels less like work and more like a calling.

As my journey progressed, I was drawn to roles that let me channel my passion for people. And today, I am grateful to wear many hats – as a corporate leader, executive coach, founder, thought leader, consultant, author and speaker – all tied by a common thread: a dedication to people.

With an emphasis on achieving results that go beyond numbers, I focus on people and purpose to build workplaces that are both effective and fulfilling. When people feel truly connected to their work, incredible things happen – not just for them but for the whole organization.

Currently, I serve as a Member of the Executive Board at Breitling and am honoured to sit on the advisory board of ICG Crimson Galleries LLC.

Switzerland is home, where I live with the love of my life, our energetic twin cherubs, and Milka, our dog. But as much as I love the mountains and chocolate, I craved a bit more adventure. It led me to an exchange year in Indiana during my teens, followed by a master's in marketing and communications in San Francisco. These experiences sparked a lifelong passion for exploring other cultures.

With more than 23 years spanning the Americas, EMEA and APAC regions, I have been fortunate to work across a variety of industries, including Luxury, Advertising and FMCG. This breadth of experience has given me a unique perspective on what drives businesses forward: people and the connections we foster.

As the founder of FlowFusion Sarl, I have developed unique approaches to foster thriving workplaces where both individuals and organizations excel. That is why I wrote a book on how to find FLOW@WORK – an approach centred on *flow leadership* and the power of the 3Ps: *People, Purpose* and *Performance*.

I believe deeply in the power of caring leadership. So, together, let us dare to care, nurture growth and plant the seeds of change that will help individuals, teams and entire organizations flourish.

This is not just about transforming the workplace; it is about creating a culture that values well-being as much as it values results. When people thrive, even the sky is no longer the limit – the stars become our destination.

Index